If the energy of heaven
does not descend and the
energy of the earth does
not ascend, then yin and
yang do not commune,
and myriad beings do not
flourish.

—Tao Te Ching

MOTHER OF THE UNSEEN WORLD

# MOTHER
*of the*
# UNSEEN
# WORLD

## *The* MYSTERY *of*
## MOTHER MEERA

### MARK MATOUSEK

Monkfish Book Publishing Company
Rhinebeck, New York

Paperback ISBN 978-1-958972-23-6
eBook ISBN 978-1-958972-24-3

Library of Congress Cataloging-in-Publication Data

Names: Matousek, Mark, author.
Title: Mother of the unseen world : the mystery of Mother Meera / Mark
    Matousek.
Description: Rhinebeck, New York : Monkfish Book Publishing Company, [2024]
    | Includes bibliographical references.
Identifiers: LCCN 2023025336 (print) | LCCN 2023025337 (ebook) | ISBN
    9781958972236 (paperback) | ISBN 9781958972243 (ebook)
Subjects: LCSH: Meera, Mother, 1960- | Spiritual biography.
Classification: LCC BP610.M422 M38 2024  (print) | LCC BP610.M422  (ebook)
    | DDC 294.5092 [B]--dc23/eng/20231025
LC record available at https://lccn.loc.gov/2023025336
LC ebook record available at https://lccn.loc.gov/2023025337

Book and cover design by Colin Rolfe

Monkfish Book Publishing Company
22 East Market Street, Suite 304
Rhinebeck, New York 12572
(845) 876-4861
monkfishpublishing.com

To David Moore

# CONTENTS

|  | Preface to the New Edition | xi |
|---|---|---|
|  | Introduction | xv |
| 1 | Becoming Mother Meera | 1 |
| 2 | What Is *Darshan*? | 18 |
| 3 | Leaving India | 23 |
| 4 | Silence Speaks | 34 |
| 5 | The Way of the Mother | 42 |
| 6 | No Guru, No Master | 56 |
| 7 | Shadow in Light | 66 |
| 8 | The Divine Life | 96 |
| 9 | The Lovers | 117 |
| 10 | Learning to Listen | 140 |
|  | Afterword | 155 |
|  | Acknowledgments | 159 |
|  | Selected Bibliography | 161 |

## PREFACE TO THE NEW EDITION

In the autumn of 1999, Daniel Siegel, a child psychologist, and author, received an e-mail from the Vatican requesting that he make a trip to Rome. Pope John Paul II, who'd recently read a book of Siegel's, wanted him to speak to the Vatican Conference on a topic of passionate interest to the Pontiff: the life-changing power of the 'mother's gaze' to a child's healthy emotional and spiritual development.

Siegel addressed the Holy See and was later invited to meet privately with the Pope, who spoke to him about losing his own mother and feeling her loss forever after. Siegel explained why the mother's gaze is so crucial—in fact, the loving attention of any caregiver can suffice—and how it anchors a person in the world. The mother's eyes communicate to a child that she belongs on this mysterious, forbidding planet. "The meeting eyes of love," novelist George Eliot called it. Siegel told the Pope that every child yearns for, and must have, this primal connection in order to thrive. These small moments of mutual rapport, transmitted thousands of times, communicate the best part of our humanity—the capacity to love—from one generation to the next. Deprived of the mother's gaze, a child may feel a like a stranger in a strange land, a wanderer in this world, unembraced by life and other people.

When I first came to meet Mother Meera, I'd never known such a loving gaze. My mother was a wounded, remote parent, and I'd felt existential dread from the earliest age, a sense of balancing on the edge of life, toes over the edge of the abyss, barely visible in a world of people who hardly knew me. Life seemed to be a cruel and selfish business it seemed and one could never depend on anyone completely. Rejection, abandonment, being forgotten could occur at any moment. A therapist informed me that my issue was a massive "mother wound" and I remember being relieved to learn that my condition was widespread and diagnosable.

When I was taken in 1985 to meet Mother Meera by my friend Andrew Harvey, I was a 29-year-old who badly needed help. A lifetime of swallowed rage and grief had hardened into a brittle shell of exhausted will. This tough persona needed to fall away so my underbelly could begin to heal. That first morning in Thalheim, after having Mother Meera's darshan the night before, I sobbed for the first time in years. In my dreams, I'd seen my puppet-like body dangling in space and being torn apart by Mother Meera in the form of a bird of prey, ripping out my entrails with her talons. Walking in the hills the next day, Andrew told me I looked better rested than I had in memory. I told him I felt as if I'd been torn open. Andrew replied, "Just wait."

Forty years that passed since that transformative day and my relationship with Mother Meera (born

Kamala Reddy), has steadily continued steadily, sometimes in the foreground, often in the background, like the percussive sound of a *mridungum* in an Indian raga. This connection between us feels outside of time; when I visit her in Thalheim, and see how gray her hair is (while I'm now bald as a bowling ball), this bond is as strong as ever. I'm aware of myself *as a soul* in her presence while Mother remains what she's always been—*sui generis*—a dependable, thoroughly mysterious source of spiritual illumination.

In the decades since our meeting, I've been lucky enough to spend time with a great many spiritual teachers, highly skilled masters and healers, but none has approached the depth or strangeness of her enigmatic power. I've had experiences around her that were rites of passage, waking visions, lucid dreams, and uncanny, inexplicable realizations. These encounters with the divine have changed me forever. Though skeptical by nature, I could never deny what had happened to me in her presence, inexplicable as these experiences might be. But to be an honest seeker truly does require a particular kind of bravery. Rilke writes about it in his *Letters to a Young Poet.*

> This is in the end the only kind of courage
> that is required of us: the courage to face
> the strangest, most unusual, most inexpli-
> cable experiences that can meet us.

To encounter Mother Meera is to cross paths with mystery, as you will learn in these pages. Many words have been used to describe her—avatar, sadguru, goddess, saint—but these are "fingers pointing at the moon" and hardly capture her ineffable power. When Mother silently takes your head into her hands during darshan, fingers lightly touching your temples, then gazes directly into your eyes—as if searching your entire being—you will know how it feels to be loved completely. To be seen and held in a steady embrace. This bond, I've learned, is unlike any other, when you can finally see yourself through the eyes of love.

I hope that this book can be a doorway to such love for you. Knowing that a Mother's gaze such as this one exists has changed my life.

MARK MATOUSEK
Springs, New York
December 2023

# INTRODUCTION

On the evening of August 24, 1984, I arrived in the nondescript village of Thalheim, a German hamlet outside Frankfurt, during a stopover from New York to India. My travel companion, Andrew Harvey, had suggested that we start our journey here with a visit to someone he was eager to see. As his guest, I hadn't inquired further, and now, as we made our way through the quiet streets, past lace-curtained windows and garden gnomes, patrolling perfectly manicured lawns, I felt jet-lagged, unanchored, and clueless as to why we were there.

Herbert, the burly, bespectacled German who'd picked us up at the airport, backed into the driveway and turned off the ignition. He instructed us to leave our bags outside and to enter the house without making a sound. *Darshan* had already begun, Herbert told us. I had no idea what he meant.

We tiptoed into the small foyer and closed the door behind ourselves. No sooner had I slipped off my shoes—following Andrew's lead—than my ears were filled with a strange buzzing sound like a swarm of bees or static on the radio. I rubbed my ears, but the whirring continued, breaking the otherwise eerie silence. I glanced at Andrew, who grinned at me, nodded his head, and gestured for me to follow him up the stairs.

Then I saw her. Peeking over the banister, I noticed a tiny Indian woman wearing a vermilion sari, seated on a chair, eyes closed, holding the head of a kneeling child between her hands. Her dark face was serene, her shoulders slightly hunched as she touched the boy's temples, the two frozen in a strange tableau. Neither of them moved a muscle. Finally, the young woman opened her eyes, released his head, and sat back, gazing straight into the boy's eyes. Her expression was fierce and unwavering, her head rocking slightly forward and back as she examined the boy for a few more seconds, then lowered her eyes, gazing down at her hands. The boy touched his forehead to the ground and returned to his chair, making way for an old woman, who hobbled to the carpet and knelt with difficulty, the whole process beginning again.

I was mesmerized by the sight of her. I knew immediately, without knowing how I knew, that this woman was unlike anyone I'd seen before—qualitatively different—as if she belonged to another species. I recognized viscerally, not rationally, as one would acknowledge a taste or a smell, that she was something *other*. Her stillness, her silence, the curve of her shoulders in silhouette, or, more than that, the atmosphere that surrounded her, reminded me of something enormous and ancient, like a mountain.

I sat down on the stairs and closed my eyes. Immediately, the background of my inner vision turned orange-gold and I felt myself sinking into a kind of trance, my body heavy, my head light. Against this glowing background, the woman appeared, floating above me in slow motion, then bouncing me through space like a seal with a ball. I was aware of being somewhere beyond myself, observing from an odd remove as she soared back and forth, teasing me, pulling me further and further from my ordinary mind.

The Baal Shem Tov, a Hasidic master who lived three hundred years ago in Poland, compared his first spiritual experience to turning around and stepping out the back door of his mind. At seven-thirty P.M. on that summer night, I stepped through the back door of my own. With no preparation whatsoever, I was shaken to the core, changed—in a matter of seconds—from a man who believed he knew the world to a person aware that he knew next to nothing.

Andrew touched my shoulder. I opened my eyes. The space in front of the woman was empty; it was my turn—she was waiting for me. I was tempted to stand up and run down the stairs. Instead, I managed to get to my feet and kneel down in front of her. Feeling awkward and ridiculous, I lowered my head, and her fingers came to rest on my temples, gripping my skull like a vise. Without intending to, my hands found her feet through the folds of her sari—they were cold and small as a child's—and I touched them as she held my head, focusing on the threads of gold in her hem. Aside from the embarrassment of kneeling in front of another person for the first time in my life, I felt nothing as I waited for her to finish. I did my best not to breathe too loudly and counted the seconds until it was over.

Finally, she released my head, I sat back on my heels and looked into her dark eyes. Her face was blank and expressionless. The irises—which nearly filled the entire oval, like a cat's—flicked back and forth as she stared at me. I had the sense that she was actually *doing* something with her gaze, focused with such intensity, as if she were boring through a wall. It took every ounce of my strength not to look away. Finally, she lowered her eyes and I returned to my place on the stairs.

The woman remained seated a minute more. When no one else came forward, she stood—bringing the small group to our feet—and made her way slowly up the stairs, eyes lowered to the ground, followed by the female attendant who had been seated at her side.

The small house emptied within a few minutes. Andrew led me down the narrow staircase to the basement kitchen and told me to wait there. My head was in turmoil; no sooner was I alone than I began to deconstruct my experience on the stairs. I was stressed, exhausted, hallucinating. I'd been influenced by Andrew's poetic descriptions of spiritual life in his native India. I was swept up by the strangeness of seeing this woman holding other people's heads in silence. I ticked off a list of rational explanations for what had happened. Andrew then poked his head through the doorway. "Mother Meera will see you now."

I followed him nervously up the stairs. The woman was standing in the foyer, flanked by her smiling companion, who introduced herself as Adilakshmi. Mother Meera was barely five feet tall and avoided making direct eye contact, a well-worn sweater around her shoulders. I tried to talk but my mind went blank. Luckily, Andrew came to the rescue. He told them I'd just arrived from America and was going through a very hard time in life. "Mother," he said, "Mark has no spiritual life. He's been diagnosed with a terrible illness. Will you help him, please?"

My cheeks burned with embarrassment. I was angry at Andrew for telling my secrets. I looked at Mother Meera, and our eyes met. She turned to Adilakshmi and said something in her native language. Her voice was deep and gravelly and didn't fit her appearance at all.

"Mother says you will sleep tonight!" Adilakshmi told me cheerfully in her singsong English. I managed to thank Mother Meera for allowing me to stay in her house. She looked at me and said, "You are welcome." Then she turned and climbed back up the stairs to her private apartment.

My first night in Thalheim, in a room directly under Mother Meera's quarters, I slept for fifteen hours. It was a sleep unlike any that I had experienced, dominated by graphic, vivid dreams. Mother Meera appeared as she had on the stairs, floating around in various costumes, changing color, shape, and size. First, she was pink and stroked my head gently, cradling me against her soft breast. After that, she turned a demonic red with bulging eyes, protruding fangs, and gnarly claws like a bird of prey's. There was blood dripping from the side of her mouth as she savagely tore at my belly, ripping my entrails out with her talons. In the dream, I screamed and clutched my stomach, struggling to protect myself, but finally surrendered to her fury. Mother Meera continued to attack me until I was left gutted, floating in midair, like a doll with its stuffing torn out.

When I woke up, Andrew had his arm around me and I was crying like a baby. He sat with me while I sobbed for a long time, curled up under the blanket. A grief no therapist had come close to detecting had been released, the hardness in my solar plexus pouring out in spasms. Afterward, I took the first easy breath that I could remember, and felt as light and clean and fresh as a child.

·

That afternoon, Andrew and I walked in the woods above Thalheim, following a footpath that bordered a pasture dotted with grazing cows. Afterglow from my morning ordeal had left me feeling wonderful. We sat on a bench overlooking the valley, and Andrew proceeded to fill me in on the highlights of Mother Meera's story. The daughter of illiterate farmers, she'd been born Kamala Reddy in the South Indian village of Chandepalle on Christmas Day 1960. An introverted child, Kamala was also independent and fearless. "She was never close to her family," said Andrew. "Sometimes, she'd wander into the forest at night by herself. They'd find her sitting under a tree." Kamala was afflicted with strange physical symptoms as well. "No one knew what to do to help her," he told me. "She would run these high fevers and scream out in pain." Since Chandepalle had no local doctor, Kamala's parents were left with no choice but to watch their daughter carefully and pray that she would recover from these episodes.

The most serious "illness" came shortly after her sixth birthday, when, with no warning whatsoever, Kamala appeared to lose consciousness for an entire day. Terrified that she'd fallen into a coma, the family made offerings to the gods to save her. At last, the girl awoke from her trance, but it would be years before Kamala revealed what had actually happened to her that day, Andrew told me. Not until a gentleman neighbor named Venkat Reddy (no relation) noticed the girl's unusual presence, and became her first confidant and devotee, did Kamala begin to describe the nature of her spiritual episodes. "She told Mr. Reddy that this experience was her first immersion in *samadhi*," Andrew said, explaining that *samadhi* is a state of intense concentration regarded as "the final stage of union with the Divine." A tiny percentage of advanced yogis and mystics attain *samadhi* after a lifetime of practice and devotion, he told me. Kamala had reached this enlightened state spontaneously, at the age of six.

"In India, it's common knowledge that rare individuals come into the world fully conscious of their divinity," Andrew went on. As an agnostic, I admitted to not being quite sure what he meant by "divinity." "Think of it this way: If creation is a spectrum of being, as physicists and mystics tell us, with the lower lifeforms at one end and human geniuses at the other, individuals like Mother Meera exist at the farthest point of this spectrum. They are spiritual geniuses of the highest order. In India, we call them the *avatar*, meaning of divine descent. Not that they descend from heaven, but that heaven, or God consciousness, descends fully realized with them. Mother knew who she was when she was born." Andrew explained that every avatar comes into the world with a unique mission from God. "That's why they call them divine incarnations. Christ came to teach brotherly love. Buddha came to teach the end of suffering. Mother Meera is here for a different reason."

"What is that?" I asked. But Andrew had said enough. We sat on the bench for a long time, gazing out at the peaceful vista. A spotted eagle swooped overhead. A fawn and its mother nosed through the sorghum grass. An enormous red bull dozed alone in its pasture. In the distance, Andrew pointed to a pair of brightly dressed figures strolling along the lane that bordered the outskirts of Thalheim. It was Mother Meera and Adilakshmi on their way to the cemetery to visit Mr. Reddy's grave. Both of them were carrying flowers.

In the days that followed, I watched Mother Meera like a hawk, waiting for some misstep, some indication that she was not the enlightened being Andrew claimed she was. But I could find no evidence that she was a fake. Whether giving *darshan* or walking to the bank, she was the same—self-contained, modest, and strangely noble, like a peasant queen.

She terrified me.

Outside of *darshan*, I did my best to avoid meeting her on the stairs or in the garden. When I crossed her path, I looked away and couldn't speak. To make matters even more confusing, Mother Meera did not act like a guru. She did not spend her days on a dais surrounded by flowers, having her feet oiled. As Andrew had explained, she gave no formal discourses; nor did she dispense advice. She made no rules, created no dogma, belonged to no religion, allowed no ashram to form around her. When people wished to dedicate their lives to her, Mother Meera would tell them to go home and keep the faith that they were born into, and return for *darshan* when they wanted her help. Apparently, Catholic priests and rabbis came to visit. Buddhists, Hindus, Muslims, Sikhs, atheists were all welcome— and Mother Meera never asked for anything in return. During the day, she was always working, mixing cement, hauling bricks, hammering shingles on the roof, sweeping the porch, watering flowers. Completely ordinary except for this strange silence that seemed to surround her.

I convinced myself that Mother Meera was some kind of *lusus naturae*, a freak of nature, like those people with enlarged pineal glands who reportedly move iron carvings through glass with their fingertips. There was no doubt that she was extraordinary. What I did question was the outlandish claim that she was a divine incarnation, or avatar, in conscious communication with God. As a nonbeliever and skeptic, I had a life-long aversion to credulousness, taking things on faith, or believing in anything I had not experienced myself. I made an agreement with myself that if Mother Meera really was the spiritual genius Andrew claimed, a representative of a higher order, that I could be as skeptical as I pleased and the truth would win out anyway.

On the day we left for India, Andrew asked Mother for a private *darshan* to bless us on our trip. She came downstairs in her work clothes, sat on her chair, then took our heads in her hands, staring for longer than usual into our eyes. Afterward, she stood up and said, "Have a safe journey."

Andrew left me alone in the room. There were two portraits behind Mother Meera's chair, one hanging to either side: a photograph of her as a teenager with a large red *kumkum* dot on her forehead; and a painting of Mr. Reddy, round-cheeked and smiling in his white Nehru cap. I stared at the images for a long time, then had the unexpected impulse to lay my head on the cushion where Mother Meera had been resting her feet. After making sure that no one was coming, I knelt down quickly in front of her chair and placed my forehead on the white pillow. Immediately, my ears were filled with the same electric, buzzing sound I'd heard when we'd first entered Mother's house. I stayed there for a long time, listening. "Show me who you are," I said inwardly. "I need proof."

When I lifted my head from the cushion, my skin was burning.

How do you respond when your mind encounters phenomena it can't seem to explain? The uncanny, the mystical, the otherworldly? What is the intelligent response when your once-solid wall of reason cracks, offering glimpses of an unseen world, a dimension you did not know existed? Scientists confront these shocks of the real on a regular basis, of course, when the windows of perception—what they take to be reality—are shattered in the laboratory or through the lens of a telescope; when the mysterious secrets of this little-known universe suddenly reveal themselves. Similarly, mystics throughout the ages, conducting experiments in expanded consciousness, have reported that what we perceive through our physical senses, and take to be reality, is a tiny sliver of what actually exists in the quantum field through which we are moving. Just as peering through a microscope or telescope opens our eyes to the infinitesimal or cosmic picture, the presence of enlightened mystics is said to reveal a landscape both intimate and unfamiliar, a luminous realm akin to our everyday world but foreign, too, with its own extra-sensory coordinates. In her classic study *Mysticism*, the scholar Evelyn Underhill tells us why these rare individuals ought to be treated with the same respect we reserve for people of science. "Mystics are the pioneers of the spiritual world," she writes, "[and] should claim from us the same attention that we give to other explorers of countries in which we are not competent to adventure ourselves."

Since meeting Mother Meera three decades ago, and spending time with other spiritual masters, I've come to agree with this view unequivocally. I've seen and felt too many inexplicable things not to understand how little I actually know. This is indeed the most important choice a person makes in a lifetime: To open our eyes to the unseen world or screw them shut in denial or fear? To kill spiritual experience with cynical logic or remain curious, flexible, willing to learn—aware that we comprehend a tiny fraction of what there is to be known—in the way that scientists, adventurers, and artists are called to? In his *Letters to a Young Poet*, Rainer Maria Rilke described this perennial challenge:

> That is at bottom the only courage that is
> demanded of us. To have courage for the
> most strange, the most singular, and the

most inexplicable that we may encounter. That mankind has in this sense been cowardly has done life endless harm; the experiences that are called "visions," the whole so-called "spirit-world," death, all those things that are so closely akin to us, have by daily parrying been so crowded out of life that the senses with which we could have grasped them are atrophied. To say nothing of God.

When I admitted to Mother Meera, a few years back, that I don't believe in miracles, she smiled and said, "What appears miraculous to man is logical in the eyes of God." This echoed a conversation I had with Spyros Sathi (the Daskalos), one of the greatest Christian mystics of modern times. "Orthodox science today knows very little about life," the eighty-year-old Cypriot told me. "You call such incidents miracles. No. They are phenomena occurring within the mercy of the absolute superintelligence we call God." Perhaps. The questions nevertheless remain: How is an ordinary person to understand descriptions of a world we know so little about? How are we to make sense of (or peace with) the existence of divine reality, if such a thing truly exists? What are we to make of Mother Meera and her kind, individuals who palpably transmit a numinous, transformative power? In order to tell Mother Meera's story, and address these mysterious questions, I've taken the empirical approach pioneered by Christopher Isherwood in his biography of Ramakrishna, the renowned nineteenth-century saint. "This is the story of a phenomenon," the novelist warned. "I only ask that you approach him with the same open-minded curiosity you might feel about any highly unusual human being, a Julius Caesar, a Catherine of Siena, a Leonardo. Dismiss from your mind, as far as you are able, such categories as holy unholy, sane insane, wise foolish, pure impure, positive negative, useful useless. Just say to yourself as you read: this, too, is humanly possible."

•

A few provisos before we begin. In writing about Mother Meera, I've avoided interpretation wherever possible, allowing the facts to speak for themselves, and included only those things I can back up firsthand, was told by Mother Meera herself, or learned from reliable sources within her intimate circle. I've been faithful to terminology commonly used to describe who Mother Meera is and what she is doing—terms such as "avatar," "Paramatman Light," and "Supramental consciousness," which may strike the reader as strange at first but will soon become familiar. Every spiritual personality comes into the world with her or his unique identity, and this cultural background affects their work in the world as well as how we see them. Mother Meera is no exception and I did not want to denude her story of foreign terms and details for the sake of Westernization. The peculiarities of a holy person's life are part of their paradoxical existence, higher consciousness shining through a unique human form with particular habits, tics, and contradictions—just like every one of us. As Mother Meera explains in this book, it is this intersection between the divine and the human, embodied by the incarnation, that points us to the truth of our own godly nature. Keep in mind that although Mother Meera is an Indian woman from a Hindu family, her spiritual power transcends culture. The force coming through her is no more Indian than $E=mc^2$ is German physics.

Still, as a South Indian woman of a certain age who hails from a traditional background, Mother Meera—an extreme introvert—resists invitations to engage in intimate self-revelation. I've never met anyone less besotted by the precious details of what makes her herself. When an acquaintance of mine asked Mother what she sees when she looks in a mirror, her reply confirmed this ("What I see is not interesting to me"). It is extremely challenging to write about someone so devoid of self-cherishing, I quickly learned. As a journalist, I've interviewed a wide range of difficult people—politicians, movie stars, global scoundrels, hermits, visionaries, and actual legends—but no one, a fraction as elusive as Mother Meera. The private details included here—Mother's pet peeves, her least favorite foods, her relationship to the physical body and emotions—are offered less for idle interest than to give the reader a keyhole view into the personal experience of a self-proclaimed avatar, and how this God-in-a-body thing works.

When I asked Mother Meera for permission to write this book, I admitted that there must be many others more qualified than a guru-phobic, nonbelieving Jew from New York City. She didn't seem the least bit concerned. "Write the book you want," she said. "Some will believe. Others will not. Leave the rest to God."

That is what I've decided to do.

1

# BECOMING MOTHER MEERA

*Before coming here, I*
*knew who I was, knew*
*that I would incarnate,*
*and what my work would*
*be.*

—MOTHER MEERA

To understand how Kamala Reddy became Mother Meera, let us travel back to Chandepalle, the village in South India where she was born. Chandepalle is a lackluster town resembling thousands of other whistle-stops across the vast subcontinent. While the population has grown in recent years, and glass-and-stone office buildings have filled in the empty lots, Chandepalle remains what it was back in December 1960: a backwater community of shopkeepers, farmers, and petty officials whose operations line the Vinukonda-Darsi Road. Strolling along the dusty thoroughfare, you're likely to pass groups of men smoking clove cigarettes in the shade, shooting the breeze and drinking tea while mangy dogs linger in the dirt for handouts. The air will assault you with the acrid smells of fried food and incense, wood smoke and flowers, excrement, diesel fuel, and garbage. You'll pass sidewalk temples whose dark interiors flicker with the light from butter lamps, their altars lined with marigolds and figurines of Hindu goddesses—Kali, Durga, Saraswati, Lakshmi—deities worshipped in South India for thousands of years before the birth of Jesus, as facets of the Divine Mother.

Heading east off the Vinukonda-Darsi Road, you will come to the boarded-up bungalow where Antamma and Veera Reddy lived at the time of Kamala's birth with their two small children, a boy and a girl under the age of five. The tiny stucco home, with its thatched roof, was divided into three parts: a living space, a *puja* room for prayer, and a storage area cordoned off with a muslin curtain. Although the Reddys were not especially religious, they kept images of the Divine Mother on the altar to bless their home, as a Christian family might hang a crucifix on the wall, more from convention than piety.

On the night Antamma went into labor, additional garlands were placed on the altar to ensure the baby's safe arrival. The pretty young mother-to-be had endured a miserable pregnancy. A few weeks earlier, racked with pain, Antamma had been carried by bullock cart to be examined by the doctor in the nearest town, some twenty miles away. The pain had hardly abated, and all were concerned for Antamma's health and the safety of her unborn child. Now, as the hours of contractions wore on, Antamma lay on a cot in the storage area, attended by women from the neighborhood, who kept pots of boiling water on an open fire and stayed nearby throughout the night. Veera listened to his wife's cries, unable to help—delivery rooms were the female province—praying that she and the baby would survive.

A few hours past midnight on Christmas Day, Antamma gave birth to a baby girl. Too weak to feed the infant herself, she entrusted the child to the care of a friend, but not before giving her a name meant as protection in her mother's absence—Kamala, meaning "divine light" and "lotus." The baby's first meal is said to have consisted of warm goat's milk dripped into her mouth from a seashell.

Over the next few years, Kamala showed herself to be an unusual child, sickly but strangely self-assured, with a stubborn, independent nature. Her siblings both adored and were distant from her. Kamala behaved like a child sometimes—singing songs and playing games—but was often quite unreachable, preferring to do her chores alone. In time, Kamala's sisters and brothers (ultimately the family included six children, four girls and two boys) treated her less as a peer than as a beloved, mysterious sister they looked up to: smart, helpful, but hard to fathom. Kamala would often accompany her mother into the nearby forest at dawn, where Antamma collected banana leaves, *patravali*, to be sold as serving plates. Kamala sometimes sat in the shade for hours on end without moving or uttering a word before returning with Antamma in the early evening.

Although there was a school in Chandepalle for kids eleven years old and under, the Reddy family could not spare the children's help in the rice fields, so Kamala and her siblings were not taught to read or write. Kamala had little interest in book learning in any case, preferring physical labor and time outside in nature. When the neighbor kids returned from school and Kamala's sisters joined them for their studies, she would go her own way. Quick-witted and observant, she had a prodigious appetite for work in spite of her diminutive size. Nevertheless, the physical episodes that afflicted her might overwhelm Kamala at any moment: attacks of fever, fainting, and extreme pain that caused her to lose consciousness. The worst of these attacks came when Kamala was six years old and fell into the open-eyed trance that lasted an entire day. As Andrew described it to me, this was her first experience of *samadhi*, a spiritual initiation that taught her "complete detachment from human relations." A short time later, a holy man from a local village told Antamma that her daughter would live far away and help many people in her lifetime, and that "everything she touches will turn to gold."

·

When Kamala was eight years old, she was sent to work as a servant in the home of the wealthy family who lived next door. The Reddys (no relation) owned the rice fields where her parents labored, as well as the bungalow they lived in. A high cerulean-blue wall stood between their mansionette and the hut belonging to the poorer Reddys', dividing their social universes. On one side of the wall there was poverty—shared beds, meals of dal and rice eaten from leaves on a dirt floor—while next door sumptuous dinners were served

on china at a mahogany table. Unable to feed his grow-
ing family, Veera sent his hardest-working daughter
to serve in his boss's home for a few extra rupees a
month; she supplemented the family income by doing
household chores. Kamala seems to have enjoyed the
relative calm of the Reddy home, so unlike the rambunctious, crowded place she'd grown up in. Her new
employers were taken with her dependable, agreeable
nature and Kamala's quiet ability to get things done. In
time, they came to treat her like a daughter.

When the head of the wealthy household died, the
Reddys were thrown into turmoil. A large estate with
no male heir on the premises is unheard-of in India
to this day. The family's only candidate was Venkat
Reddy, the lofty-minded son-in-law, and a most
unpromising choice for the job. At forty-two, Venkat
had only two interests: social activism and spiritual
seeking. His passion for God had begun early in life. "I
would cry for the Divine Mother when I was a boy,"
he later told Adilakshmi. "Since my earliest childhood,
for as long as I can remember, I was looking for her. In
dreams I used to see the face of a young girl with large
dark eyes. That was the Mother I was looking for, I
knew, but not how to find her." Venkat's longing for
this Supreme Mother was so extreme that he nearly
committed suicide on three occasions. Eventually, he
was able to channel his desperation into the fight for
India's independence, working with Vinoba Bhave,
a renowned revolutionary and an ally of Gandhi's.
While on a fund-raising trip in the provinces, Venkat
happened to knock at the door of his future father-in-
law, who grew so fond of the passionate young activist
that he later offered him his nine-year-old daughter's

hand in marriage. Bowing to family pressure, Venkat married the girl, who was half his age, with the proviso that the legal arrangement not interfere with his spiritual calling.

Leaving his child bride in Chandepalle, Venkat quit politics, gave away his family inheritance, and set out in search of the Mother of his dreams. First, he visited Mannikyama, a holy woman who lived in a hilltop cave near Venkat's hometown. "Mannikyama greeted me in silence," he later recalled. "We meditated for twelve hours without a break, and she asked me to stay with her. But I knew that Mannikyama was not the Mother I was looking for." Venkat learned of another female saint, Chinnamma, and eventually spent two years living in her hut, to the great consternation of his family. Chinnamma finally sent Venkat away, explaining that only the company of Adi Parashakti herself, the Supreme Mother, would satisfy his soul.

At last, Venkat found his way to Pondicherry and the ashram of the great yogi-scholar Aurobindo Ghose. Sri Aurobindo was a Cambridge-educated sage who combined ancient wisdom with a radical, futuristic vision of human evolution in a teaching he called Integral Yoga. When Venkat arrived at the ashram gate in 1950, the great man had recently died and the community was now presided over by an extraordinary woman called Sweet Mother. Born an Egyptian Jew in Paris, Sweet Mother (née Blanche Rachel Mirra Alfassa) had been Aurobindo's spiritual consort for half a century, having first come to India with a mystical calling at age twenty-one. With her kohl-shadowed eyes and dramatic head scarves, Sweet Mother was a sibylline matriarch, adored by the ashramites and, soon enough, by Mr. Reddy, who remained in Pondicherry for nearly fourteen years. Though Sweet Mother was not the Adi Parashakti Mr. Reddy had yearned for since childhood, hers was a powerful feminine presence that satisfied his maternal longing. When Sweet Mother died, at age ninety-five, the year before Venkat was called back to Chandepalle, he had no intention of ever leaving the Aurobindo ashram, which had subsequently become home to his wife, himself, and their toddler daughter.

When news came of his father-in-law's death, Venkat was devastated. The idea of abandoning the seeker's life for that of a gentleman farmer was ludicrous. He lacked all managerial skills and had no interest whatsoever in commerce. Traveling home by bus, he tormented himself with thoughts of what might be coming. To make matters worse, he had to leave his wife and daughter behind at the ashram during this transitional time. Feeling like the man who fell to earth, Mr. Reddy stared out the bus window hour after hour as it dragged its way across the plains of Andhra Pradesh, not knowing that his life was about to implode.

●

Mr. Reddy's sister-in-law had arrived early at the Chandepalle bus station. She'd brought Kamala along to carry the luggage. Kamala looked forward to meeting the prodigal son, whose letters from the ashram were often read aloud to the family. Having seen photographs of Kamala at that age, I can picture her waiting there at the bus stop, standing apart from her well-dressed employer, a barefoot eleven-year-old girl wearing a simple cotton sari, her thick black hair braided down to the waist, a faraway look in her feline eyes. Did Kamala know what was about to happen? Mother Meera confirms that she did. "Mr. Reddy handed over the suitcase to me. Then he asked,'Who is this girl?'He stood there, staring, like a statue without blinking. With so much love in his eyes." Mr. Reddy described a similar astonishment: "Kamala had the same face as the girl in my dreams. I wandered all over India, and found what I had been looking for in my own home."

Despite their vast age difference, the relationship between Mr. Reddy and. Kamala quickly blossomed. His family began to worry about Venkat's inordinate interest in the pretty pubescent servant girl. Unfazed by their criticism, he spent increasingly more time conversing with Kamala as she worked, asking questions about her life. Mr. Reddy insisted that she should not be working there but ought to be living in an ashram or a monastery. Kamala seemed to enjoy his conversation. It was the first time in her young life that anyone had expressed interest in who she was, truly. In time, Kamala came to trust Mr. Reddy, whom she recognized from her own premonitions as the dark-skinned man wearing a white dhoti who would help her in this life.

After his wife and daughter arrived from the ashram, this budding relationship became intolerable to the family. Attention once lavished on his daughter, Jyoti, had been transferred manyfold to Kamala. The more convinced he became of the girl's transcendental nature, the more intense Mr. Reddy's infatuation grew. Tensions reached a breaking point when his wife sent Kamala to work in the home of a Sikh family in Hyderabad without her husband's consent. Mr. Reddy was furious, but this brief separation served an important purpose. Forced to leave her patron's side, Kamala had the opportunity to show Mr. Reddy what she was made of, spiritually speaking. This is how Mr. Reddy described it to Adilakshmi:

> She had gone to stay fifty kilometers away. I was lying on my bed one evening. I heard her voice calling me and was amazed. How could she come all that way? I got up and looked for her. I could not find her anywhere. Later, I went to the city where she was. Mother said to me, "I came to you and you did not notice anything. I called out to you and you didn't hear." I asked her how she had come that far. She just said that there was another way of traveling.

When Kamala returned from Hyderabad, the situation went from bad to worse. Though she did her best not to antagonize the family, she could do nothing to prevent Mr. Reddy from following her around or singing her praises to anyone who'd listen. Observers blamed Kamala for his entrancement and came to believe that he was possessed. Suddenly, she was the enemy, rejected by the family who'd embraced her. This soap opera reached its climax when Mr. Reddy's sister-in-law slapped Kamala across the face for some minor offense. Apparently, Kamala ran from the house and disappeared into the rice field where her father was working. Mr. Reddy pleaded with Kamala to return, but her days as a servant girl were over. Offended by the assault on their daughter, Kamala's parents resigned from their jobs on the spot and made plans to hire themselves out as temporary workers. Kamala told Mr. Reddy that it was not her destiny to work this way and that she would be visited by "many people in the future."

·

Mr. Reddy kept a small farmhouse for himself in a secluded spot near the forest a few miles from Chandepalle, and it was here that Kamala began to spend most of her time in the months following the incident. Away from the prying eyes of family, she and Mr. Reddy were able to speak openly about Kamala's identity and the details of her spiritual experiences. "She knew she could tell me everything because I believed her," Mr. Reddy told Adilakshmi. "She could trust me. She knew I would do everything I could to help, protect, and prepare her." Kamala described traveling through astral worlds, encountering divine beings, gods and goddesses, as well as "supramentals" with elongated bodies and translucent skin. "Those were the happiest days of my life," Mr. Reddy said. "Sometimes, Mother would wake me in the middle of the night to tell me where she had been and what she was doing. She would sit at the end of my bed and tell me everything, what the gods had said to her, what lessons she had learned, what amazing and beautiful sights she had seen. So simply and with such childlike wonder. I came to understand who she is."

Antamma and Veera were troubled by this

unconventional friendship but did nothing to stop their daughter from spending all her time at the farmhouse. They were witnessing the fruition of the spiritual nature they'd seen in Kamala since childhood: the trances, fits, and strange behavior. She told Mr. Reddy that she had been visited, since the age of three, by "different lights" that became her teachers. Kamala had never needed her parents' guidance, and now, when Antamma and Veera visited the farmhouse, it was as if they weren't even related. On days when Kamala was in *samadhi*, Antamma and Veera were instructed to sit in the front yard, along with the other visitors from the neighborhood. According to Mother Meera, these trances became open-eyed in time, as Kamala learned to maintain this state of intense concentration in the midst of ordinary life.

●

As these masterful powers revealed themselves, Mr. Reddy became ever more convinced that Kamala belonged in a spiritual community where her presence could be fully appreciated. He dreamt of introducing her to the elders of the Aurobindo ashram. Since the death of Sweet Mother, there had been no spiritual leader in Pondicherry, and Mr. Reddy believed that Kamala could fill that role, despite her youth and the ashramites' loyalty to their deceased guru. Blinded by his own affections, Mr. Reddy was unaware of how very naïve this notion was. He was a man on a mission, having become persona non grata after leaving his family in Chandepalle, where he was universally mocked as a heartsick buffoon. "People say I gave up everything for her," he told Adilakshmi. "But this has been my greatest joy."

The plan to introduce Kamala to the ashram elders in Pondicherry began to take shape. First, he would take Kamala to a sanctuary place for a time of preparation, nearly two hundred miles away in Mahbubnagar. Then they would travel to the Aurobindo ashram, where he hoped his teenage protégée would be recognized as the great soul she was, and welcomed with open arms. Like a mother fussing over her debutante daughter before her presentation at court, Mr. Reddy worried over Kamala's appearance, outfitting the girl in silk saris and *khussa* (homemade embroidered shoes), placing gold bangles on her slender wrists and jasmine blossoms in her hair. He instructed her in how to eat Western-style and to properly address strangers. These ministrations were mostly unnecessary; not only was Kamala self-assured and naturally graceful, but her innate ability to read other people far surpassed Mr. Reddy's. She apparently enjoyed his loving attention and indulged Mr. Reddy's need to play her protector, something she would do until the end of his life.

Finally satisfied with Kamala's progress, Mr. Reddy took her by train to Pondicherry on February 28, 1974, settling them into a borrowed apartment near the ashram. Strolling along Pondy's immaculate streets, Kamala told Mr. Reddy that she felt at home for the first time in her life. This experience of home-coming was confirmed when they visited the tomb shared by Sweet Mother and Sri Aurobindo. There, Kamala was personally welcomed by the mystic couple in a vision she later shared with Mr. Reddy:

> I went to the tomb and did *pranam*. I
> could see clearly how the bodies of Sweet
> Mother and Sri Aurobindo were laid in
> the tomb. I saw Sri Aurobindo as a young
> boy surrounded by members of his fam-
> ily. And then I saw Sweet Mother and Sri
> Aurobindo waking up, as if from a trance.
> Sweet Mother walked to a chair under a
> tree in the ashram and sat down. I ran to
> her. Sweet Mother caressed me, took me
> into her lap, and blessed me. She handed
> me the flower "Prosperity."

Mr. Reddy began to introduce Kamala to his ashram friends, who were impressed by the teenager's
quiet presence but unmoved in their loyalty to Sweet
Mother. The only exception was Adilakshmi Olati, a
well-born young woman who had been Mr. Reddy's
ward at the ashram. Adilakshmi had been eager to meet
the mysterious farm girl who'd so captivated her mentor in Chandepalle. Like Mr. Reddy, Adilakshmi had
come to Pondicherry against the wishes of her family
and with a fervent desire for spiritual life. Having finished an MA in philosophy, Adilakshmi was bound for
a suitable marriage when, at nineteen, she slipped out
of her parents' house and made her way to the railway
station in her hometown of Madanapalle. Adilakshmi
intended to catch a train to the city of Poona, where
she hoped to become a disciple of a famous guru there.
At the station, she handed her money to the clerk at
the ticket window and was "accidentally" given a train
ticket to Pondicherry when the clerk "misheard" the

destination. In a movie script, this plot twist would be too coincidental to be believable in light of what came later. Yet according to Adilakshmi, this is precisely what took place.

In her book, *The Mother*, Adilakshmi describes this convergence of unlikely circumstances. "I had to find God or die," she writes. Years before meeting Kamala, Adilakshmi had intimations of encountering a Divine Mother to whom she could dedicate her life. "I had heard her name before I met her and felt, for no reason I can explain, that she was very close to my heart," Adilakshmi continues. "We in India do not think of the gods and goddesses as far away. They are all around us. They walk our streets, they come to us in dreams." On the afternoon Mr. Reddy brought Kamala to Adilakshmi's bungalow for tea, she recognized the girl immediately as some form of divine being. "Her spiritual power was obvious to me," Adilakshmi explained. "I never had a single doubt." This devotion has never wavered, in fact. "People always ask me, how do you know that Mother is divine?" she goes on in her book. "Well, I have lived with her for thirty years! I see her sometimes for twenty-two hours of the day. I am not a stupid, love drunk person. I watch, I observe. I know she is absolutely unlike me. Do you imagine I would give up my life to her had I not known?" Considering Adilakshmi's hardheaded demeanor, the answer would be a definitive no.

Though Mr. Reddy was eager to introduce Kamala to the ashram elders, cautious responses from his cohorts in Pondicherry suggested that such a meeting was premature. Instead, he decided to send Kamala to a finishing school at a hostel for orphan girls near

Hyderabad. Though she had no earthly desire to study, or any need for such "finishing," Kamala once again allowed him to play Pygmalion to her Galatea. These eighteen months at the girls' hostel would comprise Kamala's only formal education (though it was Adilakshmi who would later teach her to read and write). Cramped by the school's curriculum, Kamala endured classes in sewing, cooking, and home economics in order to please Mr. Reddy. She seems to have been popular with the headmistress and her fellow students, and was a quick study, but she kept to herself at the hostel, much as she'd done back home in Chandepalle.

In fact, Kamala was about to embark on an education of a very different order. On December 12, 1974, she had an experience in which her body was introduced to an intensified form of spiritual energy. This is how she described it to Mr. Reddy. "I was not in good health for ten days and did not know what to do," Kamala reported.

> Then I slept and heard a voice say, "Ask for the *darshan* of Paramatman." I did not know that Paramatman was the Supreme Lord. My heart drove me on and a Mother appeared to me and asked me, 'Where are you going?' 'Mother,' I answered, 'I heard a voice and I am going to Paramatman.' The Mother didn't say anything.
>
> At dawn I woke up. I was not well. I slept again from seven till midnight. My whole body was shaking with pain and fear. Then I heard a voice as loud as thunder, as if it

were being made by thousands of people. When I woke up, I saw I was alone, and said, 'Paramatman, I don't know who you are and I have never even heard your name. Don't trouble me like this because if I stay in this condition I'll die in a few days.' I waited to see if the pain would return.

After six a.m., I saw Paramatman's dazzling light. At eight a.m., I woke up and my body felt much better. After this experience, I knew why my body became weak and tired. It was because it knew that Paramatman's light was going to enter in.

This appearance of the Paramatman Light signaled Kamala's readiness to offer the light to others in *darshan*, which she did for the first time after leaving the hostel and returning with Mr. Reddy to Chandepalle. One day while sitting outside the farmhouse, Kamala was asked by a passing neighbor if she would give him her blessing. Kamala instructed the man to kneel in front of her; then she took his head between her fingers, held them there for a minute or so, released his head, and stared for another minute into his eyes. Later asked about the origin of these gestures, the same ones she uses in *darshan* today, Mother Meera says simply, "They came."

Not long after, Kamala had a dream in which she was visited by the goddess Durga—among the most powerful female deities, the wife of Lord Shiva in Hindu scriptures—who explained, "The girl Kamala is henceforth to be known as Mother Meera." This instruction came with an additional message to be passed along to Mr. Reddy: he was not to leave her side for a moment. "Mother would go into *samadhi* for fourteen hours without a break," he said. "She would eat and sleep very little."

Her true work in the world, as Mother Meera, had begun.

2

# WHAT IS *DARSHAN*?

QUESTION: *In darshan,*
*do you always use the*
*Light to do your work, or*
*do you also work in some*
*other way?*

MOTHER MEERA: *It*
*is through the Light alone*
*that my help comes.*

*Darshan* is a Sanskrit word meaning "presence" or "manifestation of the Divine." In India, *darshan* is most commonly used to describe being in the company of a holy person, an encounter that focuses, heightens, and intensifies the spiritual consciousness of the devotee. "The constant flow of love and light which emanates from [great beings] makes an irresistible appeal to the inner feeling of the aspirant, even when he receives no verbal instruction from them," explained Meher Baba, another self-proclaimed avatar (1894-1969).

Silent himself for the last thirty-plus years of his life, Meher Baba used only an alphabet board to communicate. "Man has had enough words," said that great Parsi master. "I came not to teach but to awaken."

Mother Meera communicates through silence as well, speaking directly to the hearts of those she meets, cutting through the chattering, turbulent mind. "In silence, you can receive more," she assures us. "The true experience of bliss is beyond words."

While the *darshan* ritual appears simple from the outside, the process itself, as Mother Meera describes it, is surgically complex. When she holds our heads in her hands, this is what she claims to be doing:

> On the back of the human being is a white line running up from the toes to the head. In fact, two lines start from the toes, rise along the legs, join at the base of the spine and then become a single line reaching to the top of the head. The line is thinner than a hair and has some knots in it, here and there, which divine personalities help to undo. When I hold your head, I am untying these knots. I am also removing other kinds of obstacles from your spiritual practice.

Directing this Light through her fingertips, Mother Meera describes accelerating our spiritual progress by untangling these energetic knots during *darshan*. With these obstructions removed, the light is free to rise in the body. "When I touch your head, the light moves upward in the white line," she explains.

It indicates, like a meter, the development of your *sadhana*. When there is no progress, the light moves downwards along the line, showing the degree to which your *sadhana* has deteriorated. When the light is continuous from the toes to the top of the head, the person may have many experiences and visions, although some people have visions and experiences without this white line. When the line gets to the top of the head, people have the Paramatman *darshan*. When the line has gone above the head, then there is a constant relation to Paramatman.

When Mother Meera releases our heads, she stares directly into our eyes. This second part of *darshan* appears to be more exploratory in nature.

I am looking into every part of your being. I am looking at everything within you to see where I can help, where I can give healing and power. At the same time, I am giving Light to every part of your being. I am opening every part of yourself to the Light. When you are open, you will feel and see this clearly.

Mother Meera's *darshan* prompts drastically different reactions from different people. Responses range from sublime to neurotic, peaceful to disturbing, grateful to angry, liberating to confused. I heard three first-time attendees at *darshan* tell dramatically contrasting stories over a two-day period. A thirty-five-year-old bank teller from Heidelberg reported that when she looked into Mother Meera's eyes, it felt as if she were "drowning in a sea of color and light." An American attorney nearing seventy, wearing an Hermès scarf and diamond earrings, admitted that encountering Mother Meera had roused her darkest shadows. "As if I were smeared with something terrible," she said. "All this shame came up to the surface. I went back to my hotel room and sobbed afterward, feeling like she'd seen the monster in me." (The second night, she reported being "filled with love.") A forty-two-year-old chemist from Haifa, decked out in dreadlocks, a yarmulke, and an Eminem T-shirt, told me that he felt split in two. "My lower half was all lit up, energized. Actually aroused," he said. "But my upper half felt like I'd been hit with a brick. Especially my head."

Others, like myself, tend to feel very little during *darshan* yet have extreme aftereffects (the space between my ears seems to vibrate like an empty barn after a tornado). These responses to *darshan* are wholly subjective and have nothing to do with any difference in what Mother Meera is offering. "Reactions depend on the children who take, not on the Mother who gives," she points out. "*Darshan* is completely impersonal on my side. I give what is needed." Mother advises us not to pay too much attention to our subjective fantasies: "Try not to impose your difficulties on me or project on me your own hidden problems. There is no such thing as a bad *darshan*." Her only suggestions for optimizing the experience are openness and receptivity.

*Darshan* invites us to practice what Sufis call "lunar" attention, rather than our usual "solar" attention. The lunar view is more trusting and relaxed than the solar, where energy is beamed out from the eyes to project power and dominance. Lunar attention relaxes our defenses and allows us to welcome the outside world in. Such openness can seem counterintuitive in a culture where power is prized and vulnerability undervalued; when you're led to believe there's a lot to hide, the prospect of being seen *completely* can seem terrifying. Nonetheless, it remains our deepest human longing to be seen without judgment for who we are, recognized for our essential goodness, free of shame and self-defense, exposed, accepted, and blessed without condition.

There's an enlightening parable told in India that illustrates this universal longing. The insecure seeker is compared to a child sobbing in his mother's lap. The mother strokes the child's head and rocks it against her breast with infinite love and infinite patience. Finally, the child stops crying and gazes up into the luminous eyes of the mother who is holding him. The child feels her radiance and begins to sense, for the very first time, who and what he actually is, the progeny of this great mother, joined to her in body and spirit, never abandoned and never alone. When she smiles, the child learns to smile, too. And in that moment of silent love, he knows that he has found his way home.

# 3

# LEAVING INDIA

When Kamala arrived in Pondicherry for the second time, as Mother Meera, her fame began to spread. Dr. Bhose, the ashram physician, was called in to examine her and was so impressed by the fifteen-year-old that he suggested the ashram leaders come together to meet her for themselves. This interview took place in the home of Arabinda Basu, a close disciple of Aurobindo's, and was attended by a handful of silver-haired seniors wearing spotless white kurtas and *dhotis*. As Adilakshmi reports in her book, *The Mother*, a reporter for the national news agency UNI was also present.

At first, the elders were primarily interested in Mother Meera's visionary encounters with Sweet Mother and Sri Aurobindo. "Do you feel their presence always?" Basu asked. "Or do you feel that they appear before you on occasion?"

"Always," Mother Meera said.

"How do you know that they are Sweet Mother and Sri Aurobindo?"

"They introduced themselves to me," she told them.

"And what are their forms?"

Mother Meera described them as "resembling their physical forms" but "full of energy and light which take different forms." Her answers seemed to arise with no forethought or conjecture. There was no attempt to convince her audience that she was telling the truth. Startled by her focus and self-assurance, the men went on to ask Mother Meera questions about her own life. "Why do you not get rid of all your physical troubles by higher forces?" one of them wondered, knowing of her bodily symptoms.

"When I am in Supramental consciousness, I forget about them," she answered.

"What do you feel when the Supramental forces descend?" asked another.

"The body becomes light, instead of heavy. Supermind is full of light, knowledge, peace, power, and bliss."

Basu himself chimed in. "By answering are you thinking?" the old man inquired.

"It is not possible to speak with the mind," she replied. "I see things and tell about them."

Asked if she was able to give knowledge, bliss, and light to others, Mother Meera answered, "If they are ready to receive then I can give to them."

"Do you want to be a yogi or great person?"

"No," Mother said.

"And do you want to change particular people or the world?"

Mother Meera told them, "The world."

The interview continued for over an hour. After they were through with her, the elders reported that

Mother Meera's responses seemed to come "from somewhere beyond her education," that they'd seen "nothing to discredit the claim that Mother Meera is an avatar" and had, in fact, "heard things suggesting that the claim might possibly be true."

Following the publication of the UNI story, letters began pouring in, Adilakshmi remembers, "begging Mother's help with every conceivable problem and difficulty." Soon the three of them moved into a larger house at 47 rue Manakula Vinayagar Kovil, and Mother began offering public *darshan* for the first time. She asked that portraits of Jesus and Mary be hung on the wall next to those of Sweet Mother and Sri Aurobindo, as a welcoming gesture for Western visitors. In those early days, Mother sometimes agreed to answer questions after *darshan*, and in no time these meetings attracted international wisdom seekers traveling the subcontinent. Among the first foreigners to receive *darshan* was a young Quebecois named Jean-Marc Fréchette, followed shortly thereafter by Andrew Harvey, whose memoir about Mother Meera, *Hidden Journey*, would play a significant part in her reputation spreading in the West.

Also among these first visitors were Herbert Bednarz and Daniel Toplak, a pair of European seekers who would later make it possible for Mother Meera and Adilakshmi to settle in Germany. Daniel and Herbert talked to me about those early days in Pondicherry. "What was Mother like?" I asked Daniel. We were kicking back in his messy bedroom on the second floor of the house he still shares with Mother Meera and a handful of other old-time devotees in

Thalheim. A sleepy-eyed Slovenian with a wry sense of humor, Daniel spends his days doing artwork and cleaning out roof gutters for a living.

"It's not so easy to describe," he told me in his tentative English. "Sitting there with the *darshan*, I was feeling somehow—how do you say it? Electricity. Some kind of light. There were only four or five of us there, and Mother was so young. Still, she was the same as she is today," he said. "Always the same."

"Do you see Mother as a divine incarnation?"

Daniel chuckled. "I didn't know what the Mother was in the beginning. Only that I was feeling somehow happy when I went away from her. There was a lot of sweetness. I could feel myself falling into a kind of ecstasy. I knew that Mother is the real thing." Without having answered my question, Daniel communicated what mattered to him.

I met Herbert in the garden later that day. His experience of those early days was very different from Daniel's, I wasn't surprised to learn. "We had to wait two weeks in Pondy before she finally came in a taxi," he said of that first encounter. Herbert is a fast-talking German with a forceful demeanor, known both as a loner and as the bruiser you want on your side in a fight. "Mother had gone to stay in her village. To be honest, I was not so sure about this Mother Meera. Friends had told me about her, but I'm not really one to believe what I hear." Herbert winked and raised his eyebrows. "I was becoming interested in spirituality at the time. Whatever *that* was. I had heard about this Mother Meera and came to Pondy to see for myself. We were standing on the opposite side of the road, waiting for her. She got out of the taxi and turned around and smiled at us. When she looked at me, it hit me. Bam!" His face lit up at the memory. "Whatever it was, I was blissed out. Everyone else was, too. A few days later, we had *darshan* and Mother answered a few questions afterward. She spoke in Telugu, and Adilakshmi translated. One person asked, 'Mother, why do you give *darshan* in silence?' She told him, 'Talk you can get anywhere.'"

I asked Herbert how he would describe Mother Meera's effect on his spiritual life. He puzzled over this for a moment. "The process has always been the same for me. I have a little opening"—Herbert gestured as if unscrewing the top of his head—"then I feel a strong longing in my heart. The tears are coming after that, usually, and bringing a very strong peace, sweetness, and joy. There are no questions and no special lights or anything. Just something clear inside."

•

Eager to bring Mother to the West, Jean-Marc and his fellow Canadians invited her to give *darshan* in Montreal later that year. Mother Meera left India for the first time in late August 1980 and flew from Chennai to Montreal; she, Mr. Reddy, and Adilakshmi would remain there for the next four months. *Darshan* was offered in the home where they were staying, and once a week at the Masonic Memorial Temple for as many as three hundred people a night. The Canadians' reactions to *darshan* were characteristically varied and subjective. According to Adilakshmi, "Some saw the Mother as the Virgin Mary. Others saw her as Jesus or Buddha. Others experienced the Light in different colors—white, blue, gold, orange, violet—according to their development and need." The Mother Meera Society was established in Montreal during this visit, with strict instructions that it not become a religious institution.

The threesome left Canada in January, made a stopover in Switzerland at the request of some new European devotees, and then returned to Pondicherry. As Mother's popularity increased, so did the intensity of her experience with the Paramatman Light, which appeared to be transforming her physical body in startling ways. As she told Mr. Reddy in *The Mother*, "The Light entered into my body through my fingernails, like a procession of ants."

> I saw the Light pass physically through my fingers. When the Light entered my body, it was shaken as if by an earthquake. My sense organs were cut off and I could neither see nor hear. I felt the whole process as one of complete cleansing. It was impossible to control my body. My body also became helpless. I felt as if I had no bones or nerves and I felt my heart going weaker. I could not pick up any objects, they just fell out of my hands. I could not walk and I felt as if my knees and not my feet were standing on the floor. My body was as weak and supple as a snake and I couldn't stand upright. It seemed to me that it became very light and no longer was on this earth. When the experience ended, the whole body remained painful for two days,

although my mind and heart went immediately back to normal.

There were more dramatic episodes to come.
Mother described this continuing illumination: "The
Light is bursting out from me as a great tremendous
sound like thunder and dazzling, bright sunlight. I am
sending Light like this everywhere three times a day.
When the Light leaves my body, it leaves with such
an enormous sound that I cannot hear for two hours
afterward. This process is going on."

These attacks left her body feeling like "an empty
bottle being shaken with the Light" and like "a liquid
rising, falling, moving in all directions." Her convul-
sions were nearly unbearable to watch. "It was as if
her whole body was being annihilated. She was somewhere—we do not know where," Mr. Reddy later
recalled in *The Mother*. "If we called her, she did not
answer. All the functions of her senses were stopped.
The entire body was shaken, legs and arms moving in
all directions."

Mother Meera stopped eating and sleeping
during this period. Afraid for her life, Mr. Reddy and
Adilakshmi wanted to call a doctor, but Mother Meera
forbade it, telling them that "no one can help." Her
body seemed changed afterward. "It gave the impression of having become as soft as velvet. Shining," Mr.
Reddy remembered.

It was during this time that Mr. Reddy's own body
began to fail. He'd been ignoring several chronic ail-
ments for years, and his diabetes had become life-threat-
ening. The European devotees, including Daniel and
Herbert, invited Mother Meera to Germany before her

second visit to Montreal. By the time the plane landed in Frankfurt, Mr. Reddy was dangerously ill (though he tried playing down his condition). Making their way from the airport to the town of Essen, in Daniel's car, Mr. Reddy dozed in the front seat while Mother Meera and Adilakshmi sat in the back, enjoying the wintry landscape. At one point, Mother turned to Adilakshmi and said in Telugu, "There is something here." The portent of these words was unclear for some time.

Daniel welcomed his guests into his small home, moving his own bed into the cellar to make room for them. Members of the Transcendental Meditation (TM) Society were especially eager to meet this young avatar and flocked to the house in the coming days. The founder of TM, the Maharishi Mahesh Yogi, had been shown Mother Meera's photograph, apparently, and encouraged his followers to seek her *darshan*. "The Divine Mother is in Germany and it is a good thing," the guru assured them, according to Herbert.

In Essen, Mother Meera and Adilakshmi spent the afternoons exploring the local shops and buying groceries for dinner, to be prepared in Daniel's make-shift kitchen. "Mother would cook the most delicious simple meals," Daniel told me. "None of us had any money. Nobody minded chapati and rice. We were just so happy to have Mother here."

After three weeks, Mr. Reddy was so sick that they were forced to abort their stay in Germany. It was decided that they'd make a brief visit to Montreal before returning to Chennai. This plan was not to be, however. While they were in Canada, Mr. Reddy's health collapsed, and when the government failed to offer him urgent treatment, there was no choice but to fly back to India immediately. Scrambling to change planes in Frankfurt, Mr. Reddy went into kidney failure and the German authorities offered to give him free dialysis if he wanted to stay in the country. Despite his protests, Mother Meera insisted that he begin treatment. Mr. Reddy would never set foot in India again.

Herbert found them a place to stay in Kleinmaischeid, a town on the outskirts of Bonn. Three times a week, Adilakshmi rose at four A.M. to prepare breakfast for Mr. Reddy before the ambulance took him for treatment at a hospital in Bonn. In the afternoons, Mother Meera would help him back up the stairs to his bedroom. On December 26, the day of Mother's twenty-first birthday, a dozen devotees gathered to celebrate while Mr. Reddy watched from his place on the sofa, each guest receiving *darshan*. As Daniel remembers it, "Mother held our heads for twenty minutes at a time in those days. She used to say,'The first minute is for me and my work. The rest is for you.'Who knows what she meant? We were very happy."

When Mr. Reddy's dialysis failed, he was moved to the hospital in Bonn, where he remained for the next six months. Day after day, Mother Meera looked after him as his health continued to decline. "The Mother was feeding him with her own hands," Adilakshmi wrote in her book. "She stayed in the hospital late hours at night caring for him." It was at that time that Mother Meera declared openly that Mr. Reddy was a "special being who had come for a special purpose." While the doctors offered no hope, his condition eventually improved enough for him to leave the hospital, though the question of where they could put down roots had not yet been resolved. Mother Meera and Adilakshmi had been forced to vacate their temporary home, but although they were offered free lodging by the TM group, Mother declined. Instead, with Mr. Reddy's encouragement, she made a down payment on a house with the help of the German devotees. Daniel cosigned on the mortgage. "We just worked and saved, worked and saved, so we could get the house ready in time for people to come for *darshan*," Daniel recalled of those penniless days. "We gave up everything that costs money. Beer, television, cigarettes." Adilakshmi pitched in by selling hand-painted lampshades at the marketplace in nearby Limburg. The shades were decorated with stenciled flowers and tassels made by Mother Meera herself.

By April, the house was ready for visitors. Though Mr. Reddy was released from the hospital that month, he could no longer leave his bed. While Mother Meera gave *darshan* in her own home for the first time, he lay upstairs, heartbroken not to be at her side. Withdrawn from the world, Mr. Reddy "went towards the Mother," according to Adilakshmi. "There was a rapid inner development in him. All the parts of his being were concentrated on the Mother alone." Mother Meera would call him by his pet name, Gundu, meaning round and complete, and he'd smile like a child and become emotional. Sometimes, she'd tickle him till tears of laughter rolled down his face and he begged her to stop.

On June 14, Mr. Reddy's health declined further. He asked to hear his favorite devotional songs of India;

afterward Mother fed him and helped him to bed. The next day, he entered the hospital for the last time. Five days later, Mr. Reddy was gone. The death of her closest confidant, the first person to recognize her and be trusted with the details of her spiritual experiences, who'd given up everything to devote himself to her work in the world, prompted a grief in Mother Meera unlike anything she had displayed before. "When he left his body, the Mother felt that some part of her was divided from within her," Adilakshmi wrote. "This feeling was too painful to put into words. I saw and felt whenever I touched her, that sorrow was flowing from her like a river."

To express this sorrow, Mother Meera picked up a paintbrush for the first time and, over the next three months, created a series of portraits depicting Mr. Reddy's soul voyage after death. She painted directly, without making any kind of a sketch, producing one new picture each day. These extraordinary images, later collected into book form *(Bringing Down the Light)* offer the only visual testament we have of the world through Mother Meera's eyes. Mr. Reddy's soul is depicted as a translucent sheath, flowing and pale, surrounded by towering, multicolored figures representing Divine Mothers, with strange tadpole heads and a single oversized eye, who look down on his diminutive form. In the final painting of the series, Mr. Reddy's soul—portrayed in a pale shade of purple—is being safeguarded by three Mothers, who are gathered at its side, holding its head and feet with bunches of flowers in their hands. His soul had reached the end of its journey.

# 4

## SILENCE SPEAKS

When Mr. Reddy died, Mother Meera settled into a quiet life in Thalheim for the next six years, rarely venturing out of Germany. The arrival of an Indian holy woman in this sleepy Catholic village was tolerated remarkably well by her neighbors, some of whom sent their children to Mother's house to receive her private blessing. The mayor of Thalheim came to Mother Meera with a liver complaint and is said to have been cured. The parish priest came for *darshan*. From her ordinary lifestyle, it was clear to her neighbors that this was no exotic cult. Passing her modest home, neighbors might find Mother Meera hauling bags of cement across the driveway or pounding shingles into the roof, and were greeted with a friendly smile. The influx of visitors from around the world brought revenue to local businesses as well, which didn't hurt her popularity, either.

Unlike most Eastern masters coming to the West, Mother Meera refused self-promotion and gave no interviews, preferring the quiet life of a private citizen in her adopted country. In fact, Germany was more to Mother's taste than India had ever been. The weather was blessedly cool, for starters—Mother Meera dislikes the heat—and with its emphasis on efficiency, cleanliness, and order, the German work ethic pleased her more than the catch-as-catch-can style of India. Here she was free to move around as she pleased without fanfare or unwanted attention. In India, even in those early years, it was hard for Mother to venture out in public without devotees dropping to her feet in *pranam* or assaulting her with garlands of flowers. In Thalheim, there was no such hoopla. Locals who encountered Mother Meera and Adilakshmi walking to the grocery store or visiting Mr. Reddy's white marble gravestone greeted the foreign women politely and went on their way without making a fuss.

This period of reclusion was interrupted in the fall of 1989. After years of Andrew's pleading with Mother to give *darshan* in the United States, she agreed to offer three public meetings in New York City and a question-and-answer session at Hobart and William Smith Colleges, in upstate New York, where Andrew was on the faculty. I had seen Mother only once since our first meeting and was especially eager to be there for her first interview in the United States, particularly in an academic setting. On the day of her arrival at JFK Airport, I was with the small welcoming party waiting at the terminal. Andrew paced back and forth, watching the information board and holding a bouquet of white roses. The rest of us were scattered around the arrivals lobby, on the lookout lest we miss Adilakshmi and Mother Meera somehow.

At long last, the customs doors opened, and there they were. Mother Meera looked petite and slightly disheveled, her purple sweater half-buttoned over a navy blue sari, handbag slung over her shoulder, with Adilakshmi at her side, scanning the room for familiar faces. When Mother saw Andrew, her face lit up; he touched the flowers to his chest and offered them to her with tears in his eyes. We followed the three of them to the baggage carousel, and when one of us managed to ask Mother Meera how she was feeling, she simply replied, "I am fine. And you?" That was the extent of the conversation.

The following afternoon, a few dozen academics and students gathered in the colleges' wood-paneled library for the interview. The group was diverse, ranging from tweedy professors to undergraduate girls wearing midriff-baring tops and short shorts. To my right, a teacher corrected student papers, turning to her friend at one point to say, "This isn't really my thing. But Andrew is *very* persuasive." I felt protective and apprehensive all of a sudden. Had it been a bad idea to invite Mother Meera into the brain-heavy halls of a highbrow American college, unschooled as she was? The bar of doubt might be too high, I feared, the intellectual rift unbreachable.

At three o'clock exactly, the door opened and Mother came in with Andrew and Adilakshmi close behind her. Without being instructed to do so, the attendees rose to their feet all at once, and Mother made her way to the front of the room, settled into a chair, and tucked a tissue into her sleeve. She was wearing a cream-colored sari trimmed with iridescent green, with four gold bangles on either wrist, and looked more beautiful than I'd ever seen her, closer to sixteen than twenty-nine. Andrew delivered a glowing introduction, during which Mother avoided eye contact with the audience and Adilakshmi grinned at the people in the front row. As Andrew offered the highlights of Mother Meera's life and the basics of *darshan*, I sensed the crowd beginning to listen. The teacher next to me took a notebook out of her bag. After Andrew finished speaking, Mother closed her eyes and that eerie quiet fell on the room. We sat together in pin-drop silence for a full three minutes. Then Mother opened her eyes, nodded at Andrew, and the interview began.

Andrew asked the first question: "Mother, I'd like to start by asking if you always knew you were an avatar?"

"Before coming here, I knew who I was," she said in her deep, incongruous voice.

"You have said that you are not a human being, Mother, although you are in a physical body. What do you mean?"

"Although there is a human form, I have never been born a human being," she replied. Her tone was matter-of-fact. "There has never been any separation between me and my divine identity."

The woman next to me scribbled "incarnation?" in her notebook. Andrew invited questions from the audience, and an elderly gentleman wearing a bow tie raised his hand. "Mother Meera, I am a practicing Christian and also a professor of religion," he said. "In my faith, we are taught that there has only been one divine incarnation, Jesus Christ. And he was a man."

"That is false," Mother said.

The professor looked unconvinced. "There are many intellectuals who have no faith," he went on. "They claim that God is dead or never existed. I work with several of them at this school."

"They may think that they have no faith," Mother Meera answered. "But everybody believes in something." The old man looked delighted at this, as if she'd confirmed what he, too, believed. The professor smiled, and she smiled back.

A student in a bright yellow peasant dress raised her hand. "Why do you give *darshan* in silence?" she asked.

"When people have a silent mind, they will receive more. For the mind to flower, it has to go beyond what it knows."

Now it was my turn to ask a question. "Don't we need the mind for discernment?" I asked, confused by the role of the mind in spiritual life.

"Both the mind and the heart must accept God," Mother told me. "First you must accept with your mind. Then belief grows in the heart."

"I thought it was the other way around."

"First the mind must be pulled down," she explained. "Then the heart can open completely to God. If the mind does not accept, there is always doubt. The mind creates every problem. Not the heart."

Several people raised their hands at once, and over the course of the next half hour, Mother responded to a range of questions, from why she lives in a German village ("To show the world that the transformation is normal and can be done anywhere in daily life"), to the special focus of her work ("To bring the Light to human beings"), to her attitude toward human resistance ("Let people receive whatever they can. There is no desire to give"), to the difference between the Mother's way and the patriarchal approach to God as taught in Western religions. "The Father is stricter,"

Mother Meera said. "The Mother is more loving, patient, and accepting. I have come to say that all paths are as good as each other and all lead to the divine. Believers should respect each other's ways."

A punked-out kid in skateboarding shorts asked how Mother Meera could give *darshan* to everybody, including people who'd done bad things. Mother told him that, meeting someone in *darshan*, she sees "not one person there but many persons behind." "The whole picture must be considered," she said. "My love is for all."

This prompted my neighbor to raise her hand. "I'm curious about the soul, Mother Meera. Are you able to see a person's soul?"

She looked at the teacher and said, "Yes."

"What does it look like?" the woman asked.

Mother gazed at her for a moment. "It is a combination of light and shadow, resting inside your body like another body."

A palpable buzz went through the room. My neighbor's companion spoke up then. "Can you really help people become enlightened?"

"Yes," Mother replied with a smile. "But first you must be *ripe*."

After that, Mother Meera seemed to withdraw her attention. The questioning came to a natural stop. Mother gazed down at the floor in front of her as late afternoon light streamed through the library windows. Nobody moved for several minutes. Eventually, Mother Meera looked up, removed the tissue from her sleeve, and rose to her feet. We stood up once again as a group and watched her make her way to the door, followed by Adilakshmi and Andrew.

The next night, Mother gave *darshan* at the Cathedral of Saint John the Divine, on the Upper West Side of Manhattan. In attendance were James Parks Morton, the Episcopal dean of the cathedral, and a number of religious leaders, including a Muslim imam, a Tibetan *rinpoche*, and a well-known Reform Jewish rabbi. I found it comforting to watch Mother give *darshan* to representatives of different faiths in that institutional setting, surrounded by stained glass windows and Christian iconography. In the lobby afterward, I overheard a conversation between two young men who were meeting Mother for the first time. They were talking about how shy she seemed, "like she didn't want to be noticed at all." "I felt like she knew me," the first one said. The second boy had a different take. "When I looked into her eyes," he told his friend, "all I could see was sky."

On her last day in Manhattan, Mother visited the Statue of Liberty, which seemed to delight her (she enjoys sightseeing). That night, she offered *darshan* to a private group of a hundred New Yorkers at an opulent apartment on Fifth Avenue filled with enormous golden Buddhas and beveled mirrors as tall as trees. I brought two dear friends along to meet Mother, both of whom experienced dramatic healings after having *darshan*. One of my guests, a chain-smoker who'd been unable to kick the habit in thirty-plus years, spontaneously lost the desire to smoke and didn't pick up another cigarette for a full three months. My second friend, who was fighting a terminal illness, received an even greater blessing. For the past few months, she'd been suffering from debilitating migraines that no doctor had been able to medicate away. After placing her head in Mother Meera's hands, my friend felt her pain abate almost immediately. She returned to her seat, looking flushed and dazed, and instantly fell asleep. Ten minutes later, she opened her eyes, and the headache was almost gone. For the next four months, she remained virtually pain-free, and the day my beloved friend died, peacefully in her own bed and clutching her small wooden rosary, she told me that Mother Meera was with her and that she was not afraid.

# 5

# THE WAY OF THE MOTHER

Drive five hours south from Thalheim on the A3 motorway, across the Rhineland and into Bavaria, and you'll come to the ancient city of Augsburg, founded by the Romans in 15 B.C. and home to the Catholic church of St. Peter am Perlach, an elaborately spired cathedral located in the center of town. In the church's dark interior, near the transverse arch, hangs an eighteenth-century canvas, *Mary, Untier of Knots*, painted by Johann G. M. Schmidtner. In the baroque painting, the Virgin Mother is pictured standing on a crescent moon surrounded by angels. Above her halo of stars floats the Holy Spirit in the form of a dove. Mary is dressed in a scarlet robe with a purple stole, her eyes are downcast, and she's crushing a serpent beneath one bare foot. In her hands, she holds a length of knotted pale ribbon held up at each end by cherubs, their tiny wings the color of fire.

Mary, Untier of Knots, is the archetype of a cult from the Catholic Church dating back to the early Middle Ages. As one facet of the Divine Mother, she combines patience with ferocity, the delicacy of her healing hands matched by the force of her snake-crushing foot. The parallels between Mary, Untier of Knots, and Mother Meera's approach to *darshan* are fascinating and obvious. Night after night, year after year, Mother sits on her chair untangling the energetic knots she finds in people who come to see her, beginning with the white lines that run up our bodies in the front and back, and freeing the light to flow upward within us. In the Catholic tradition, Mary's task is to loosen the bonds of ignorance and selfishness that bind us to the sins of our fall from grace. Mother Meera uses different terminology to describe a similar process of removing obstacles that stand between human beings and our awareness of the divine nature we share with God.

Of course, the worship of the Divine Mother dates back to traditions far older than Christianity. She has been revered as the feminine face of God, "the fertile womb which gave birth to everything, the great cave of being from which she brought forth the living and into which she took the dead for rebirth," as Anne Baring, a renowned Jungian analyst, puts it. She is honored in songs that were sung by the first peoples of Alaska, Africa, North America, and Polynesia. The Divine Mother appears in Homer's hymn to Gaia, in Sumerian poems to Inanna and Ishtar, in Apuleius's vision of Isis as recorded in *The Golden Ass*, and in ancient Tibetan prayers to Tara, as Baring points out. She is the Hindu Shakti, the energetic driver of the universe, who brings to the world what Hildegard of Bingen termed *viriditas*, the verdant, electric force that animates the whole of creation.

To our great impoverishment, the Sacred Feminine has been excluded from our image of God in Western culture. For the past three thousand years, the

Abrahamic traditions—Christianity, Judaism, and Islam—have offered no image of the Divine Mother as an equal counterpart to God the Father, no union of masculine and feminine principles into a wise and balanced whole. Among many of today's spiritual leaders, there is strong belief that an integration of the divine feminine into our worldview is urgently needed if we are to heal our planet's woes, eradicate fundamentalist terror, and restore a unifying, feminine vision to our worldly affairs. Until we reintroduce the wisdom of embodiment as symbolized by the Divine Mother into our global conversation—a wisdom deeply rooted in the earth, while God the father looks down from the sky—our future is thought to be perilous indeed. As Aurobindo himself put it, "The future, if it is to exist, will wear a crown of feminine design." This would seem to be a foregone conclusion in our aggressive, polarized era.

No archetype is more powerful in the human imagination than that of the Divine Mother. Since everyone has a mother, we share the sacred memory of our primal connection to the universal feminine. This collective memory helps to explain the profound effect that representatives of the female divine, including Mother Meera, have on our sense of spiritual connection. A mother alone has the power to bring the light of a soul into the world. Her body contains the eternal mystery, the capacity to create life, and in denying her spiritual importance, we disregard a fundamental aspect of our existence; we sever ourselves from our primordial source, the matrix that nourishes the cosmos and mediates the harshness of God the father.

As a philosophical path, the way of the Mother is nonjudgmental, inclusive, and free of man-made opposites that appear to divide the world in two—sacred-profane, physical-spiritual, holy-unholy, and so on. Rather, it invites a holistic awareness that welcomes our faults as well as our strengths, promotes an attitude of surrender to life as it is, and marks the first step toward genuine wisdom. Surrender is a sign of strength in the Mother's way, bowing to forces greater than we are. Vulnerability, in this view, is the doorway to freedom. "Like a child at peace in the womb of the Mother, the realized person knows," Mother Meera says, "that he is sustained at every moment by the grace and light of the Divine Mother. Being peaceful and being happy are the foundation of spiritual life."

How antithetical this is to the notion of human existence as an ongoing, painful effort to redeem ourselves in the eyes of God or battle our weary way back to salvation. Instead of original sin, the Mother's way focuses on original blessing that is fostered by the act of surrender. Spiritual surrender means leaning into life instead of trying to conquer it, expanding our hearts to embrace contradiction, and remembering that paradox is everything. This approach does away with false separations as well as idealized concepts of God. Everyday activities—emptying the cat box, driving to work, reading to your kids at night—are understood to be just as holy as meditating, fasting, or chanting Aum, since everything, without exception, is recognized as a part of God. No enlightened master embodies this unified vision more radically than Mother Meera. Nowhere on the planet are you likely to encounter a person of her spiritual stature dragging Hefty bags to a dumpster or commandeering a power drill. "I am not interested in founding a movement for people who do not want to work, who want only to sit around and think about what they think is God," Mother Meera reminds us. "When they are really dedicated to the Divine, there is no difference between action and prayer."

•

Although Mother Meera offers *darshan* in silence and sets no rules for devotees, this doesn't mean she provides no verbal guidelines on how to live an awakened life. In fact, two collections of her spoken responses have been published, *Answers: Part I* and *Answers: Part II*, covering a wide variety of topics of importance to spiritual seekers. Unfailingly practical and simple, these teachings are mostly lingo-free and accessible to anyone. With their emphasis on the *bhakti* path of devotion (not to Mother Meera herself but to any faith that appeals to the seeker), and on divine light as a catalyst for spiritual change, her recommendations share aspects of the Integral Yoga invented by Sri Aurobindo while being free of the scriptural references. In spite of the absence of regulations, the Mother's way is actually quite rigorous in that it places responsibility for our choices squarely on our own shoulders. Each student of this open-door path is called upon, as the Buddha put it, to "be a light unto yourself," practicing self-reliance in spiritual life.

Mother Meera's essential teachings can be distilled into a handful of suggestions.

## 1. JAPA

*Japa* is the repetition of a divine name that resonates with an individual. It is the root practice recommended by Mother Meera for spiritual awakeness and remembering God. *Japa* is more than just repeating words, she tells us, since each holy name is said to contain divine vibrations. *Japa* can be done anywhere and at any time. It is best not to focus on any particular goal when doing this practice. Simply repeat the divine name with sincerity and love. Nor does it matter what name you choose to repeat. Whatever comes easily and spontaneously, and brings a strong feeling in the heart, will be effective; nor is it necessary to stick with one divine name if another attracts us on a given day. Some devotees use "Mata Meera" or "Amma Meera" (*Mata* and *Amma* both mean "Mother"), but "Ma" is equally powerful. And others use the names of the God they worship in their respective religions.

## 3. DEVOTION

Devotion is the royal path to enlightenment, according to Mother Meera. She tells us that "if you have devotion, you will get everything." True devotion in spiritual life is extremely rare, however. As she has said, "[You] weep for lovers, money, worldly things, but rarely weep for the love of God. A tear is a door through which I can come." Longing for the Divine is essential. Sincerity and devotion are far more important than excessive or showy demonstrations of love.

## 3. SURRENDER

Surrender means offering everything to the Divine, without exception. Mother instructs us to remember that no matter how great we are, "there is always something greater—the Divine." Surrender has nothing to do with resignation or weakness. In fact, surrender is a sign of spiritual strength. It is not *what* we offer but *that* we offer that is important and changes us. "The Mother doesn't look at the gift itself; she is happy that the child thought of her. In the same way, what you offer the Divine is not important, only the love."

## 4. THE EGO

As we learn to surrender, be humble, and connect with the Divine, the ego slowly dissolves. "The ego is strong in the world but weak before God," Mother Meera tells us. In order to awaken as human beings, and realize our own divinity, we must be willing to die to the ego, knowing that only self-realization can bring lasting happiness. Discipline is key to ego death and spiritual progress. "You have to cut a tree sometimes to make it straight and help it grow," she reminds us.

## 5. SPIRITUAL EXPERIENCES

Like all authentic spiritual masters, Mother Meera warns against the temptation to become attached to otherworldly experiences. However great or small, these experiences should be offered to the Divine. If we allow imagination to construct fantasies around our experiences, we will only become more trapped in illusion. Experiences come and go, Mother reminds us. Only the real—the eternal—remains. What's more, authentic spiritual experience always humbles rather than inflates the ego. As for mediums, psychics, and oracles, she recommends economy. It is not necessary to go to "all those people," since each may offer a different solution to the same problem. "They confuse people," Mother states simply. "It is more important to do *japa* and pray to God or the Divine."

### 6. MEDITATION

Mother Meera does not recommend meditation practice for everyone, especially not children under the age of twelve. When practicing meditation, she says, it is best to be simple and unambitious, since attachment to mastery and technique can increase spiritual pride rather than destroy it. In order to receive the Light, it is not necessary to meditate, though a silent mind is helpful. Sincere feeling is far more important than rigid practices.

### 7. SINCERITY

Sincerity is a prerequisite to spiritual awakening. It is more beneficial to be sincerely doubtful than dishonestly faithful. It is better to be open, truthful, and simple about our own faults than to pretend to be better or more selfless than we are. Sincerity is connected to humility, of course. "The great man is always humble because he remembers his relationship to the Divine," Mother Meera says. Only a fool imagines that pretense leads to a deeper connection to God. That goes for financial contributions as well. Once asked why she doesn't accept money from people who come to see her, Mother answered, "When people give me money, they expect something. I don't want that. They should come to me like a mother and they shouldn't pay something because then they always expect, 'When I pay a lot then I got a lot.' Or, 'I don't have any money so maybe I only get a little bit.' That's not how things work."

8. FAITH AND DOUBT

A measure of doubt is useful in spiritual life because it helps to keep us honest. As Mother Meera puts it, "It is better when someone says 'I love God,' knowing all the hatred and doubt that is still within them. Then it means something. Then the love can grow." Dwelling on doubt is not helpful, however, because what we focus on tends to grow. Faith is a quality we cultivate through intention and sincerity. Only honesty can lay the foundation for authentic awakening and make room for the Divine to help us. "Whenever the mind has doubts, I give Light to the mind to see things clearly," she explains.

9. SELF-REALIZATION

There are many awakenings in spiritual life and no end to the process of self-realization. The good qualities of the mind can always be expanded further. It is within our power to become increasingly loving, balanced, and peaceful, and to continue to open throughout our lives. The soul, which Mother Meera describes as a more subtle body within the physical form, guides our development and is always with us, acting as a kind of protector to lead us toward our own realization. The soul has no wishes of its own; it is only a witness to accompany us on the path to our own true nature.

10. SIN

There is only one sin, according to Mother Meera, and that is "not to love enough." Sin arises when we forget the Divine, whereas remembering God serves to remind us of the good in human beings. This requires a willingness to forgive. "If we do not forgive, we cannot be called human," Mother says. Although there is evil in the world, she warns against being pulled into its orbit by fear. Even though evil forces are working against the Divine in the world, the Divine is in control. "Evil is dangerous," Mother Meera says. "But also very stupid."

## 11. EMOTIONS

According to Mother Meera, emotions are generally superficial and block entry into the deeper levels of our being. This attitude is unfashionable in the therapeutic age but typical in the East. Emotions disturb our ability to be peaceful, she counsels, and ought not to be mindlessly indulged. In the case of a challenging emotion such as anger, Mother Meera recommends that we offer it to the Divine in order not to become absorbed by it. This helps us to feel compassion for those who have harmed us and to make progress in the path of love. When hurt arises, the skillful response is to "pray for those who hurt us and send them love." This helps to alchemize our pain into joy.

## 12. INTELLECT

The mind is both a blessing and a curse on the path of self-realization. In Mother Meera's words, "If the mind does not disturb or destroy others, then it can go on doing what it may." As the saying goes, the mind is a good servant but a terrible master. The study of different paths can be useful because it gives us wider knowledge and respect for other traditions, as opposed to holding a limited, rigid view. "There is great joy for the mind in following the spirit," Mother Meera teaches. But our terrible master will lead us astray if we let it blind us with shallow reasoning. As Aurobindo put it, "The habit of analytical thought is fatal to the intuitions of integral thinking. If you follow your mind, it will not recognize the Mother even when she is manifest before you."

## 13. SUFFERING

The notion that suffering is necessary for enlightenment was created by human beings, not God, Mother Meera teaches. The Divine asks us to be happy, harmonious, and peaceful, she asserts. The majority of our sufferings are the result of ignorance and insincerity. Pain is different from suffering, of course. Pain belongs to the body, so it must be accepted. But we humans exacerbate our own pain by concentrating on it, she reminds us. Offering our pain to the Divine prevents it from turning into suffering. Happiness and spiritual growth are connected in the Mother's way. "Being peaceful and being happy form the most important foundation of spiritual practice."

## 14. RELATIONSHIPS AND LOVE

Mother Meera defines love as "doing for people what they need without expecting anything in return." Love is different from attachment, which focuses more on getting than on giving. This is especially true of romantic relationships, which, while beneficial as opportunities for opening the heart, do not necessarily move us closer to God. If two people in a relationship are really focused on the Divine and are right for each other, however, their spiritual process may be faster than a single person's. But such relationships are not necessary for spiritual life.

## 15. FAMILY LIFE

Family life, on the other hand, is an optimal place for spiritual practice, since it teaches one to be unselfish. "A calm and harmonious family is a great spiritual achievement," Mother Meera teaches, since it enables us to know ourselves as part of the human family, and to view all people as related to ourselves. Mother Meera views the decline of family life in the West as a reflection of our greater ills. "If everyone in the family is happy, then the world will be happy and we will have less problems," she maintains.

## 16. WORK

Work is the cornerstone of the Mother's way. "I do not accept that people do not work," Mother Meera tells us. "Everyone must work. I am working. This is not a time for people to withdraw from the world. It is the time to work with the power and love of the Divine in the world." Also, one type of work is no better than another. The important thing is that we work to serve others, not "mechanically, but with love." She advises that we begin our work with a prayer and offer the fruits of our labor to God.

## 17. SEX AND HEALTH

Abstinence is not necessary in spiritual life. As Mother puts it, "Some paths say that cutting vegetables hurts them but we must eat in order to survive, so it's a circle. If some people don't eat meat, they suffer. So there is suffering in any case." Though self-control is necessary, there's no use in denying our natural desires. Regarding sex, the choice to be celibate should be "made in joy not from suffering." According to Mother Meera, spiritual work is done fastest if a seeker can live without sex, but very few manage it and "for many it is dangerous to avoid sexuality before they're ready." Nor is sexuality spiritually important; according to Mother, "The pleasure generated by two persons has no spiritual meaning." What is essential is not to renounce sex but to offer it to the Divine. This holds true for all forms of sexuality.

## 18. SILENCE

Mother Meera emphasizes that silence is the great awakener. By quieting the mind, we invite the Divine to take root within us. As she told me, "For the mind to flower, it has to go beyond what it knows," and this is possible only when thinking subsides and allows a deeper knowing to occur. "There is only one real rhythm," Mother Meera tells us. "In silence, you hear it. When you live to the rhythm of this silence, you become it, slowly. Everything you do, you do to it." The importance of silence goes against the common belief that words are necessary for spiritual awareness. "People want lectures. I give them silence," she explains, adding, "I do not speak, but my force changes people completely."

## 19. GURUS AND TEACHERS

It is best to pray to God directly or through a divine incarnation, Mother Meera advises. It is important to be aware of the limitations of all human gurus, who can point the way but "cannot take you to God."

One's relationship to a guru depends on how much the guru can help a particular disciple at a particular stage of development; when feelings of peace or bliss arise in his or her presence, this indicates that the guru is authentic. At this time in history, however, when travel is increasingly available—and information about different teachers, too—it is not necessary for the majority of people to pledge allegiance to a single guru. Mother Meera is not a guru.

20. SCIENCE AND TECHNOLOGY
The increase of technological gadgets that threaten direct communication requires that we use mindfulness and discipline, to prevent the machines from taking over, she says. Advances in science and technology "should be directed from a higher consciousness to help the world save itself." The temptation to put our belief in any power other than the Divine is dangerous, Mother teaches. In order for technology to help us, "Man must have a global idea of what he is inventing, and it must be constructive rather than destructive." It is arrogant to imagine that scientific knowledge trumps spiritual awareness. Scientists are often the most humble among us, Mother Meera points out, since they're used to what they cannot see and accustomed to encountering mystery.

⁕

When we practice these commonsense principles, aspiring to wisdom instead of perfection, we deepen our connection to the world around us, and to the far-reaching effects of the Mother's way.

6

# NO GURU, NO MASTER

It was a relief to hear Mother Meera confirm that she is not a guru. Like many skeptical Westerners, I have doubts about the traditional guru-disciple relationship, with its calls for obedience, exclusivity, and unquestioning devotion. Had Mother Meera encouraged such fealty, or required any kind of compliance, I'd have run for the hills and never looked back. Fortunately, she asks nothing from devotees, rejecting all attempts to turn her into a surrogate parent or an object of worship. Unlike a conventional guru, Mother warns against a devotee's becoming too attached to her physical presence or dependent on her for decision making. "There is no need to be near my physical body. I will help you wherever you are," she assures us.

Our long-distance relationship suited me fine. Returning to New York after that first trip to India—having met Mother Meera and begun a serious meditation practice—I found myself without a job, a place to live, or much hope of surviving more than a couple of years. My health had been in a steady decline, treatments for the disease were nowhere in sight, and my doctor's only recommendation was to go out and live while there was still time.

Rather than waiting to die in the city, I embarked on the life of a dharma bum and threw myself into spiritual seeking the way a drowning man clings to the edge of a life raft. If there was no cure for my physical body, at least I could try to heal my soul, to discover what, if anything, this life meant and why I was alive in the first place. I hit the road with no time to lose and a list of urgent spiritual questions. What did we mean by God, anyway? Did anything exist of a man beyond this booby-trapped bag of bones? What about enlightenment? Was such a thing possible in the time I had left? Could raising my consciousness help me to cope with these sickening, smothering feelings of dread? Driven by these riddles, I traveled from teacher to teacher, ashram to monastery, retreat center to mind-body workshop, grabbing for wisdom wherever I found it and major credit cards were accepted.

Seeking became my reason for being. I kept a quote from T. S. Eliot in my wallet: "In a world of fugitives, the person taking the opposite direction will appear to run away." I was lucky to spend time with extraordinary teachers from a variety of backgrounds: the Dalai Lama, Brother David Steindl-Rast, Matthieu Ricard, Rabbi Zalman Schachter-Shalomi, Byron Katie, Stephen Levine, Adyashanti. I had personal conversations with Eckhart Tolle, helped Sogyal Rinpoche on *The Tibetan Book of Living and Dying*, and spent a year co-writing a book with Ram Dass. I meditated with John Daido Loori, received Ammachi's otherworldly hug, and spoke to the Daskalos, Spyros Sathi, about out-of-body travel, or "exomatosis." From these sages, I picked up invaluable clues about how to live wisely in a mortal body while knowing that you are a spirit as well.

These were traumatic, eye-opening years and the most transformative of my life. I traveled to Germany as often as possible and stayed with Mother Meera for months on end, in a room on the second floor of her house. She always welcomed me graciously and allowed me to remain for as long as I liked. Adilakshmi would inquire into the state of my health and suggest that I ask Mother for help. I never felt moved to do this, however. I was there to be blessed, not saved; I was seeking acceptance, not divine intervention. Even with Mother so close by, I rarely went upstairs to speak to her. It was enough for me to see her during *darshan*, hear her shuffling overhead, or spy on her as she watered her flowers on the terrace. I'd walk in the woods, cook meals with Daniel or Herbert, and keep to myself. Each time I left, Adilakshmi wished me well at the door and would say that she hoped to see me again. I realized she meant this quite literally.

Oddly enough, though, I didn't get sicker. The years rolled by, incredibly, and my body stayed more or less the same. By 1992, I was still in commission and realized that it was time to go home. The seeker's life had become an ongoing escape; I was running away from my life, not toward it. Returning to New York, I rented a studio apartment in the Village with help from friends and family. I did my best to normalize, to settle down and integrate. I embarked on a live-in relationship, joined a meditation group, and volunteered three times a week at a hospice, rubbing the feet of dying patients and listening to their stories. I wrestled with a memoir about mortality and awakening, and collaborated with Andrew on a book about the divine feminine (later published as *Dialogues with a Modern Mystic*). It had been our intention from the start to dedicate the book to Mother Meera, our inspiration for this project, and Andrew and I worked happily for nine months in my one-room apartment, discussing the end of the patriarchy and the spiritual health of a world out of balance.

●

The first sign that things weren't right between Andrew and Mother came with a fax from Adilakshmi, insisting that Mother Meera's name not appear in our book. This request was shocking to both of us but Andrew was truly beside himself. He'd spent years helping Mother in a variety of ways, and his memoir about their relationship, *Hidden Journey*, had introduced thousands of readers to her, many of whom later came for *darshan*. After Mr. Reddy died, Andrew had taken on the role of being Mother's ambassador to the world, and done so with unflagging devotion. Now it appeared that Mother Meera, or someone around her, wanted to distance herself from our work for reasons that neither of us could imagine. Feeling betrayed and humiliated, Andrew returned home to Paris after we'd finished the manuscript, and our book went to press without Mother's name in it. I fell out of touch with Andrew after that and I never quite understood what had happened.

Then the situation got worse. Word arrived through

mutual friends that Andrew had rejected Mother for reasons I found inexplicable. Apparently, he had accused her in print of being homophobic and a fake. All of a sudden, my old friend had reversed his belief in her avatarhood, reframing Mother as a spiritual adept who later became Mr. Reddy's "invention" and now behaved with ulterior motives. I soon learned the reason for this change of heart. Following the book-related fax, Andrew had gone to Thalheim, apparently, to ask Mother why she withdrew, and to receive her blessing on his upcoming marriage to his male partner. Rumor had it that Mother refused him this blessing and, more incredibly still, requested that Andrew leave his beau, marry a woman, and write a book about how the Divine Mother's love had transformed him into a straight family man, since being gay was "unnatural."

I was flabbergasted. I'd never felt a trace of homophobia from Mother or the people around her. The first morning we spent in her house, Andrew and I were served breakfast in our room. I'd brought many gay people to *darshan* over the years, and all of them were welcomed wholeheartedly. When a friend of mine sent Mother Meera a message, asking for help in finding a partner, Adilakshmi returned with encouraging news ("Mother says yes!"). He came to meet his life partner at *darshan* the following year, in fact. When this same friend asked Mother if she had any negative feelings about homosexuality, she answered, "How could I be against anyone for anything? You must go deep into your heart, see who you are, and act accordingly. Then what could there ever be to give up?" In truth, I'd always been deeply impressed by Mother Meera's openness to alternate lifestyles; she was, after all, a celibate holy woman from a conservative Indian background. Yet here was Andrew claiming the opposite, laying his credibility on the line after years of being her greatest ally.

As word of the controversy spread, people began to contact me, wanting to know if Andrew was right. A journalist called from a magazine, asking me if I believed him. I told her that I had no earthly idea what could have happened. Was it true that Mother Meera had turned against homosexuals? Might Andrew be making this whole thing up? Would this stain Mother Meera's otherwise unsullied reputation? Torn between my own experience and loyalty to Andrew, I realized that there was nothing to do but find out for myself. I booked a flight to Germany for later that month.

Herbert met me at the airport in Frankfurt. When I asked him what had actually happened, he smiled, shrugged, and suggested that I talk to Adilakshmi. It was all "a big misunderstanding," he told me. Herbert wouldn't elaborate.

I was in my room the following day, putting off the inevitable, when Adilakshmi knocked at the door and asked me to come up to Mother's apartment. The familiar butterflies rose up in my stomach as I followed her up the white marble stairs. Mother Meera was waiting for us on the sofa, outfitted in a housecoat and slippers. Adilakshmi pulled out a chair and I sat, facing the two of them. Mother Meera greeted me warmly, asked about my health, and gazed off into the middle distance. Nobody said a word for a minute. Then Adilakshmi launched into the subject at hand: "We are very glad you have come," she said. "Have you spoken to Andrew lately?"

"That's what I wanted to ask you about."

Adilakshmi gave a knowing smile. "Andrew is angry. But the things he is saying are not true." I looked at Mother, who barely seemed to be paying attention. "The Mother's love is equal for all. Andrew did not understand."

"I'd really like to know what happened."

Adilakshmi gave me the gist of it. For many years, Mother had trusted Andrew to speak on her behalf. As an outspoken advocate for gay rights, Andrew had been outspokenly gay, suggesting in public statements that "the return of the Mother" was especially good news for homosexuals, who could now celebrate their otherness. "People began to write to the Mother, asking if it was true that she prefers gay people," Adilakshmi said. "Some of them were very upset."

"These are simple people," Mother Meera said. "With families. It was confusing to them."

"When Andrew came," Adilakshmi continued, "we only asked that if he wishes to speak in the Mother's name, then it is better not to discuss these things. If he wishes to talk about them on his own, that is no problem."

"That's all that happened?" I asked. Adilakshmi nodded her head and a weight was lifted from my heart. Still, the question of the marriage remained. "What about asking for Mother's blessing? Is it true that he was told to marry a woman?"

"Andrew can love anyone he wants!" Adilakshmi waved away the suggestion. I speculated that perhaps there had been some hesitation on Mother's part to the particular man he had chosen. When I suggested this, Adilakshmi glanced at Mother, then back at me.

"These are personal matters," she said. "For Andrew's *sadhana*. Now I would like to ask you for something, Mark."

"Anything," I told Adilakshmi.

"Will you write an article that tells the truth? We love Andrew. He is an old friend. Will you help?" I wanted to say yes but hesitated. Instead, I assured Adilakshmi that I believed her. The room fell silent after that; eventually, after a minute or so, Mother Meera stood up and walked me to the door. I expressed gratitude for her hospitality. "You are always welcome," she told me.

"Will you write the article?" Adilakshmi asked.

I promised her to do my best.

●

In fact, I wrote nothing—not a word—to contradict what Andrew was saying. I was too confused by these conflicting stories—and too repelled by Andrew's vitriol—to reckon fairly with what had happened. I was also too much of a reporter not to remember that I was nowhere near the scene when all of this had transpired. I could never know the precise truth about what was said, the tone and innuendo, what had been distorted, misheard, badly translated, or simply unintended. Could Adilakshmi have misspoken? Perhaps. Was it possible that Andrew pushed too far or overstepped some boundary? Yes. Could Mother's resistance to Andrew's choice of husband have had something to do with the guy's character? Certainly. Did I believe that Mother Meera was homophobic? Absolutely not. It seemed clear to me that this collision between them had been a long time coming. Was it my job now to pick up the pieces? Not at all. My only responsibility was to protect the sacred relationship I had with Mother Meera. There was no need for me to dive into a pile of dirty laundry that reeked of half-truths and hidden agendas.

Still, my connection to Mother was not immune to the Andrew debacle. Our inner bond remained unbroken, but I instinctively stepped away from the conflict. Mother's photograph remained on my desk, my sense of her power remained undiminished, but I kept my distance from Germany. My personal life had radically changed as well, which shifted my attention and focus. First, I'd gotten my future back when drugs appeared to treat my condition. Next, I had followed Meher Baba's injunction to "dig in one place" (and meet God wherever you are), creating a home with my new partner and working on my writing career. I'd taken Mother Meera's advice to heart as well, and never attached to her physical presence or treated her like a guru—a detachment that served me well in those years. Our bond seemed to grow even stronger during this physical absence, in fact.

Friends in Thalheim kept me abreast of the changes in Mother's life during this period. By the early 2000s, she was traveling the world, emerging from her decades-long seclusion, because, in her words, "not everyone can come to Germany." I read about Mother in magazines, watched video footage of *darshan* online, and waited for the right time to see her again.

This finally happened in April 2006. Mother was giving *darshan* at a hotel in Connecticut, and I couldn't wait to be in her presence. When the time came, I sat in the crowded ballroom, feeling excited and nervous, the way you are before meeting a long-absent friend, hoping that they haven't changed too much. When the door finally opened and she made her entrance, I was relieved to find Mother just the same, aside from a few more gray hairs at the temples. She still lowered her eyes as she walked, avoiding the audience's gaze, then settled quickly onto her chair, folded her hands in her lap, and waited for the first head to be offered. *Darshan* was also more organized now, due to the size of the crowd; each of our rows was called one at a time, with a seated queue down the center aisle. One by one, we were asked to slide forward as the space in front of her cleared. When my turn came, her fingertips locked on the top of my head, I smelled India in the folds of her sari, and when I sat back on my heels to meet her eyes, they offered no sign of recognition. Mother stared at me for an especially long time, it seemed. Then it was over, I was back in my seat, my eyes were closed, and that eerie calm came over me, an intimation of something eternal, the long-delayed return to stillness. My mind went quiet. I could hear myself breathing. I knew there was nothing to be forgiven.

# 7

# SHADOW IN LIGHT

In the mid-1990s, Mother Meera diverted funds from Germany and bought several properties in Madanapalle, a municipality in Andhra Pradesh three hundred miles from where she was born. She intended to build schools near the town center as well as a retreat house for visitors and indigents on thirteen acres of farmland toward the outskirts of Madanapalle. Ever the frugal farmer's daughter, she is said to have negotiated a rock-bottom price for the real estate, according to an inside source, while Adilakshmi, whose family had been prominent for generations in Madanapalle, finessed the relationship with the seller. There was a problem finding a water source on the farm site after the property was purchased, causing great alarm all around. The next time Mother visited India, she looked around and suggested that the workmen try a spot a hundred yards from where they were digging. That's where they found their water source, to everyone's relief.

She chose pink-and-gray marble from Rajasthan for the floors of the main school (the Mother Meera English Medium High School), and ordered a plaque for the front gate to commemorate Mr. Reddy. On one side of the campus, a visitor finds a Hindu temple devoted to the god Shiva; on the other stands an ancient Sunni mosque, while around the corner is a Catholic retreat center, transforming Paramatman Way (the name Mother chose for the street) into a cul-de-sac of world religions. The main school was to offer a standard English school education for children aged three to sixteen, many of whom would be poor and on scholarship. There would be three levels—referred to as "baby school," "kids school," and "teen school"—and a large hall to use for *darshan* after the children had gone home. Mother Meera invited her parents, Antamma and Veera, to live on the school grounds, as well as her younger brother and three surviving sisters and their families.

Creating this school was far from easy. Ulrich Reinhold, a German IT specialist and one of Mother's closest aides, described the grueling process she'd been through, working with the locals. "Mother ran straight into a wall of *tamas*," said Ulrich. "Very, very difficult." In the Hindu energy system, there are three primary qualities: *rajas* (passion and activity), *sattva* (purity and goodness), and *tamas* (inertia or resistance to action). "Basically, no one did what she asked them to do. We saw Mother become angry for the first time."

"It's hard to imagine her angry," I confessed.

"Not anger like yours or mine, where it's personal. More like Kali," Ulrich said, referring to the ferocious, ignorance-slaying aspect of the Divine Mother. "She'd get angry when people ignored her instructions. Or wasted money. Or forgot to take care of someone. But Mother's anger would be gone like that." He snapped his fingers. "She'd be laughing and smiling in the next moment, as if nothing had happened. Mother responds to the needs of the situation, that's all. She does what's necessary to get the job done. But avatars lose their temper, too, you know."

This is an important point. Smiley-faced pictures of enlightenment—blissful, beatific, ever serene— have never been a part of Indian spirituality (or any authentic tradition, for that matter). The saintly are known to be hell on wheels when it comes to relieving suffering. Think of Mother Teresa railing against Calcutta bureaucrats who were trying to interfere with programs for feeding the poor. Or the Dalai Lama fuming privately over the Chinese occupation and the massacres of the Tibetan people. Or any of the outraged sages and prophets with which the Bible is populated, as well as the Koran, the Bhagavad Gita, and Buddhist sutras on anger and hatred. It's naïve to imagine that enlightened people are milquetoasts incapable of fiery emotion, cheek turners who never lash out when pushed beyond their limits. I've known a number of masters from various traditions, and not one of them was without a temper. Still, it was hard for me to picture Mother Meera—the most unflappable and detached of all—losing her cool over worldly matters. Ulrich proceeded to set me straight with the story of a husband-and-wife team, childhood friends of Adilakshmi's, who had volunteered to help educate the children in Mother Meera's family. In gratitude to these teachers, Mother had given strict instructions to her family that a container of fresh milk from the cows that grazed behind the school be delivered to the couple every day. These orders were carried out faithfully until once when Mother Meera was visiting from Germany and her relatives forgot the delivery. While eating dinner with her family, Mother asked about the milk and was told that the delivery had been forgotten. She stood up from the table, apparently, regurgitated her food, and went to apologize to the teachers right away, complaining that her family couldn't be trusted to carry out her wishes without her keeping an eye on them.

"She doesn't forget a thing," said Ulrich.

•

I wanted to see Mother for myself in India, and booked a trip to Madanapalle. My partner, David, and I planned to volunteer at the school, where I'd have the chance to ask Mother a number of questions that I badly needed answered. I'd spent a year trying to create a portrait of her that was true to life and free of sanctimony. Mother Meera had given me carte blanche to write whatever I wanted, but her story continued to elude me. There was a missing link I had failed to uncover and it was my hope that she would help me dispel this mystery while we were in India. Before we left for India, I telephoned Mother in Germany to remind her that I would be at the school during her monthly visit and looked forward to interviewing her there. I'd seen her on a few occasions in Connecticut for *darshan* but had spent almost no time alone with her for a number of years. "There are so many things that I need to ask you," I told her, trying not to sound like a pushy reporter. "For the book."

"Yes, yes," she said. "I am busy now."

At the airport in Bangalore, David and I were met by the driver we'd hired to take us to the school. For the next two hours, scenes of rustic India flew by outside the window: tea stands with oversized, rusty tin pots; buffalo knee-deep in flooded rice paddies; swarthy women on the side of the road, balancing great earthen jugs on their heads, dressed in bright cotton saris and flip-flops. What would it be like, I wondered, seeing Mother Meera in her native country? Those frightening dreams from the night we met, when she came at me with her talons and fangs, were carved into my memory, along with the image of my ripped-apart body, hanging in space like a gutted doll. What if that happened in real life? What if Mother Meera tore me apart for some unintentional mistake or other? How would I respond to her fury? I pulled out a copy of *Answers: Part II* and reread what she'd said about her own temper: "Sometimes I become angry while working with someone who insists on doing something his or her own way when I know it will take too much time and is not good," she explained. "But this anger which is rare arises only in work situations. I do not become angry at a devotee who does something bad to another," she promised. "I change him or her." I only hoped that this was true.

•

When we arrived at the school, David and I were met at the gate by Hilda, an anxious-looking German woman in her fifties, who stopped what she was doing to greet the new volunteers. "*Ach*, we are so busy with the children!" she said, shaking her head and looking

toward heaven. Hundreds of kids in green-and-or-
ange uniforms were streaming out of buildings, into
the courtyard. I saw a familiar face emerge from the
crowd; it was Maurice, a French devotee of Mother
Meera's whom I hadn't seen in twenty-five years. He
welcomed me with a wide grin before leading us to our
room, where he suggested that we have a rest before
*darshan* started, at seven P.M.

I sat down on the bed and peered out the window.
Beyond our terrace was an empty dirt lot. At the center of the lot was a tractor, and next to the tractor a
small tree, its root ball diapered in white fabric. Beside
the tree, a young man was striking at the earth with a
shovel, surrounded by a group of fellow workers wearing head scarves to protect themselves from the brutal
heat. He seemed to be having trouble digging the hole.
From out of the group stepped Mother Meera—so
short that I hadn't seen her at first. She took the shovel
from the worker with one hand, placed her foot on
the hilt, and plunged it into the dirt. Then she wiped
that hand on her sari, put a rag to her forehead, and
squinted down at what appeared to be a cellphone
she'd been holding in the other hand. Mother turned
and walked back toward the school, followed by a
couple of minions. It was weird that with so many
men present, it had fallen to her—a bareheaded, fifty-
four-year-old woman standing in ninety degree heat—
to start the digging on this job. Then I remembered
what Ulrich had said about *tamas* and Mother Meera's
headaches with her labor force.

•

A few minutes before seven, we made our way to the *darshan* hall on the ground floor. Next to the door was a whiteboard inscribed with a couplet from Emily Dickinson: "The truth must dazzle gradually / Or every man be blind." Inside, three dozen people were seated in an incense-scented, dimly lit room that could have held five times that many. A group of children were being led in Sanskrit prayer by a sweet-voiced, ample-bodied woman sitting to the side of Mother Meera's chair. This was the first time I'd heard music allowed before *darshan*; everywhere else, the hall is kept silent. Behind the song mistress sat Adilakshmi, whose black hair had gone gunmetal gray in the twelve years since I'd seen her last. An adorable child with a Louise Brooks bob marched up and down the aisle with the confidence of a military commander, escorting newcomers to their seats. Hilda hurried around the room, shushing people who were whispering; then she'd hold up her hands, palms pressed together in the namaste sign, as if to say "I'm a very nice person under this scowl." Across the aisle, Maurice was sitting in a row by himself, with his arms crossed, eyes closed, and bare feet splayed on the pink marble floor. In the front of the room, the school's temporary administrator, an American-born engineer named Mohan, watched over things with a tense expression, frail as a wren in his gold Gandhi glasses, slender arms clasped around his chest.

Suddenly, the singing stopped and Mother Meera walked in from the back. At a glance, she was hard to recognize as the same perspiring, loose-haired woman I'd seen an hour before in the open dirt lot. Mother seems to change physically during *darshan*—the word

that comes to mind is "condensed." Her body appears
to lose a fifth of its mass. On the street, Mother Meera
looks like many a fiftyish Indian woman with an umber
complexion and good taste in saris. In *darshan*, she's
unmistakable. Sui generis.

She settled onto her chair, and the process began.
Adilakshmi went down on her knees first and lowered
her head with some difficulty, resting it in Mother
Meera's hands. How many thousands of times had she
done this in the past forty years? What was passing
between them, I wondered, watching Adilakshmi look
up at Mother, hands folded beneath her chin. When
Mother lowered her eyes, Adilakshmi touched her feet
and made way for Mohan, who brought up a plastic
chair to accommodate disabled visitors. A mountain-
ous grandmother in a purple kurta was followed by a
ragged old Indian man, a teenage girl with a twisted
leg, and a Western lady clutching a walker. The Louise
Brooks coquette summoned those in our row to take
our places in the waiting line. I pushed forward on the
floor till it was my turn, then gazed into her eyes after
*pranam*. Not a flicker of personal recognition passed
between us. I wondered if she knew that I had arrived.

•

I was blasted awake at five A.M. by a pandemonium
of amplified prayers blaring out of the stadium speak-
ers from the Shiva temple next door. Outside the
window, the courtyard was empty except for a single
worker bent double over her pail, sweeping the ground
with a handful of straw as the school's canine mas-
cots, Ambika and Puja, lazed nearby. A flock of green

parrots perched in the mango tree behind her, and a family of monkeys picked at each other's fur on the branches near our balcony, eyeing the open box of biscuits on the dining room table.

When eight o'clock rolled around, I found Mohan in the volunteers office and was given my duties: to type English lessons from outdated workbooks and act as a hall monitor when students were moving between classes. Mohan showed me where to station myself at the top of the stairs, opposite the latrine in progress, and how to keep the kids in line when they were in transit. A few minutes before the buses arrived, I took my position on the stairs and waited. Inside the bathroom, a group of workers were already installing the plumbing. I didn't notice at first that Mother Meera was among them, overseeing the job. Fascinated, I watched as she chatted with the men, who seemed easy and relaxed in her company. Maurice came bounding up the stairs, carrying a length of plastic tubing, which he handed to Mother Meera. She looked at it and said, "This is wrong." Maurice ran past me and back down to the courtyard, grumbling under his breath.

The buses began to arrive, and then the schoolyard was swarming with hundreds of children of every imaginable shape and size, from toddlers clutching lunch boxes to their chests, smiling with mischievous, curious eyes, to young adolescent boys and girls who separated into cliques and watched one another from a safe distance—most of them decked out in their uniforms. Crowding past me on the stairs, the smallest ones paused to greet me one by one. "Good morning, Uncle! What is your name, Uncle? That is a beautiful name, Uncle! My name is Pupul!"

We'd been warned not to indulge them with conversation, which was hard to resist, and I did my best to keep the children in a single file as poor Hilda marched up and down the halls, clutching a sign that read SILENCE. Two of the volunteers, a Danish kickboxer and his gray-haired father, greeted the kids as they came through the gate, and the eight young teachers (all female but one) began to take their places for the morning assembly, dressed in the school colors. When the children had lined up in front of their teachers and the stragglers had been herded into place, Adilakshmi rang a bell to bring the assembly to order. A pretty young teacher barely out of her teens stepped to the microphone and led the student body in morning prayers. "May He protect both of us," they recited in Sanskrit, chanting slokas from the Bhagavad Gita. "May He nourish us. May we both acquire the capacity to study and understand the scriptures. May our study be brilliant. May we not argue with each other. *Aum*, peace, peace, peace." As the masses of children chanted together, Mother Meera looked down from the landing, her hands covered in plaster dust.

&#9679;

Once the children were in their classrooms, I looked for Adilakshmi and found her in the library, reading a newspaper, bifocals slipping down her nose. "Welcome to the Mother's school!" she said, warmly taking my hand. "How long has it been since I have seen you?"

"Twelve years, Adilakshmi."

She bobbled her head and offered me a chair. Adilakshmi chatted to me about the school and how hard it was to run, with a thousand students and too few qualified administrators. I asked how she had found the adjustment, settling back in her hometown after so many years in Germany. Mother Meera had asked her to remain at the school, to keep an eye on things when she wasn't there. For the first time in over three decades, Adilakshmi was living apart from Mother. "How has that been for you? Is it strange to be so far away from Mother?"

She smiled. "The Mother is always with me. She is never far away."

"Of course," I said. "But what about the physical distance? She relied on you for everything, didn't she?"

"Relied on me? Not at all!" Adilakshmi waved away this suggestion, though she'd been Mother's constant companion, helper, and watchdog for as long as I'd known them. "You can see how strong she is. It has been this way since the first day I met her. Nothing has changed."

"Really?" I asked. "But a lot has changed, no? Mother is out in the world now. Constantly traveling. All of these projects—"

"But what is that to the Divine?" Adilakshmi interrupted me. "The Mother has always worked twenty hours a day. This is nothing new. India is difficult, of course. She often gets tired. But she is not affected by these things. Not in the same way that we are."

"It's hard to understand."

"For all of us," Adilakshmi agreed. "But it isn't for us to understand. The important thing is to open to God. The rest we cannot know."

"But you knew. Didn't you?"

Adilakshmi smiled again. "It is true that I

recognized her," she admitted. "From the moment we met, I trusted the Mother. I had seen her in my dreams. It was obvious to me, how great she was. And yet, the Mother remains a mystery. Even to me."

"In what way?"

"I know her better than anyone else," she told me. "In an earthly way. But even I am aware of how secretive she is, how hidden from our human knowledge. The Mother is becoming more and more withdrawn, I think. More and more secretive."

Before I could press her further, a teacher came into the library, complaining about a problem with a student. Adilakshmi turned her attention to the matter at hand. Thinking about what she'd just told me, I wondered about this secretiveness and was struck, as always, by Adilakshmi's unwavering devotion— her ability to trust in what she did not understand. Spiritual devotion, or *bhakti*, is an enigma for skeptics like myself who lack the gift for selfless surrender. Fortunately, there are other approaches to God than the *bhakti* path for people of different temperaments. There's *karma yoga* (the path of service), *raja yoga* (the path of self-purification), and *jnana yoga* (the path of inquiry), the latter best suited for doubting types whose hearts are opened more by questioning than by faith. It's hard to imagine *bhakti* more pure than Adilakshmi's devotion to Mother Meera. It's humbling to behold such trust and easy to feel like a spiritual novice in its presence.

Once the teacher had gone, Adilakshmi turned back to me. "We will speak again," she said, then went back to reading her paper.

•

After two days, Mother had not acknowledged my presence. When I passed her on the stairs, she looked away. The last time I'd seen her, in Connecticut, she'd sent an assistant to bring me to her hotel room, and we'd spent ten pleasant minutes chatting alone. Now I'd come halfway around the world to be with her and Mother Meera had not said so much as hello. The demands on her time were great, I realized. Still, the strangeness of it could not be denied. An army of demons came stampeding in: rejection, confusion, abandonment, sadness, futility, self-doubt, and, of course, anger. My distress reached such a fever pitch by day three that I vowed to make personal contact with Mother the next time our paths crossed.

On day four, I spotted Mother Meera across the courtyard, seated in the shade with a young girl who was brushing her hair. I steeled myself to approach her but was stunned when Mother did not so much as glance in my direction. Baffled and embarrassed, I stood there with my face on fire and finally croaked out a few awkward words about how eager I was to speak to her. Mother Meera grumbled, "Yes, yes," then went back to chatting to the girl in Telugu. I skittered away, feeling abject and stupid.

I found Adilakshmi in the kitchen. "There is no worry," Adilakshmi reassured me. "She is like that with everyone! We all want to feel so special."

*"Hello" doesn't seem like too much to ask for,* I wanted to protest. Yet even as the thought popped into my mind, I saw that Adilakshmi was right. I wanted

Mother to acknowledge me *personally*. I wanted her to make allowance for our personal history and the personal effort I'd made to volunteer at her school, the way any polite person would. Ordinary people care about social graces and about assuring others that *everything's fine*. Ordinary people are insecure enough themselves to care about appearances and displays of emotional bonding. But Mother Meera is not an ordinary person. She doesn't care what others think about her; nor does she have a scintilla of interest in smoothing out our ruffled egos. My expectations were all about *me*. Also, her relationship to time itself is different from an ordinary individual's. Mother Meera doesn't seem to inhabit the same clock-watching, minute-counting, time-running-out dimension most of us live in. She appears to live closer to *nunc stans*, the timeless present, the eternal now. *Nunc stans* is closer to nature's rhythm, the cosmic rotation of planets and stars, than it is to man-made ideas about time, that ever-dwindling commodity. Notions of yesterday, today, and tomorrow are said to be free-flowing—arbitrary, even—in *nunc stans*, which is why making plans with mystics can be such a challenge. In one of his books, Eckhart Tolle illustrates this point well.

> Imagine the earth devoid of human life, inhabited only by plants and animals. Would it still have a past and a future? Would we still speak of time in any meaningful way? What time is it? The oak tree or the eagle would be bemused by such a question. "What time?" they would ask.

"Well, of course, it's now. The time is now.
What else is there?"

Waiting for Mother Meera to plan a meeting was
like waiting for the oak tree or eagle to pencil you in on
its calendar. Caught up in my ego, I might also be overlooking the possibility that Mother Meera was com-
municating with me already in ways I might be able
to sense if I could get through my emotional tantrum.

Adilakshmi seemed to pick up on my thoughts.
"You imagine that the Mother is ignoring you because
she is silent. But that is not true. Mother has allowed
you to stay in her home. She is giving you the freedom to observe her here and allowing you to write
this book," Adilakshmi said. "She is showing you
where you need to grow. Shedding light on problems
that cause you suffering. Impatience. Pride. Insecurity.
Putting light on the qualities that stand in your way.
And teaching you to trust her even when she's distant.
To trust God."

"You're probably right. But it feels terrible."

"Who said the divine was easy?" Adilakshmi
asked, chuckling. "People imagine that to be close to
the Mother is to live in a state of continual bliss. But
that is untrue. Life becomes more difficult around the
divine, not easier. The Light reveals every weakness.
Every knot that is binding us. All of our darkness
comes to the surface."

"What should I do, Adilakshmi?" I asked.

"Be patient. Try to surrender. Find out what she is
trying to teach you."

●

Describing Mother Meera as "distant" is an existential understatement. She's a complete outlier, the most enigmatic individual I have ever met. Having been an interviewer for more than thirty years, I've come to know a thing or two about drawing out secretive people. But Mother Meera is *undrawable*. When asked a question, she tends to supply just the facts, generally leaving out a riposte. Standard shortcuts to verbal connection—gossip, seduction, commiseration, breast baring (or beating)—do not work with her. Her lack of interest in small talk is quite unfathomable.

And then there's the challenge of cognitive meltdown. My mind has disintegrated on more than one occasion while trying to interact with her. I'm not alone in this; it's a common phenomenon among devotees. One psychiatrist described her personal mind melts with Mother as having her brain turned into "a fondant fancy under a grill." While sitting with Adilakshmi and Mother in their living room, with snow falling outside the window and a log crackling in the fireplace, I once attempted to interview Mother for a magazine article. In mid-sentence, my mind disappeared—simply blanked out—and I froze in my seat, unable to speak, while Mother gazed at the fireplace and Adilakshmi drifted away. The three of us sat in that deepening silence together for several blissful minutes; and then, as quickly as it had descended, the silence passed, my mind reappeared, and I knew that it was time to go. Once I'd left Mother Meera's presence, I had the clear impression that she had orchestrated this silence somehow. Rather than spend our time together discussing philosophical questions, she'd given me what I truly wanted: a glimpse into the world she inhabits, a taste of what the divine world feels like: soundless, mysterious, vast, and profound, underscored by a pulsating wonder.

Now, in Madanapalle, I did my best to tune in to her frequency and decode what she might be saying to me with her silence. My confusion reminded me of a story about the Buddha. Near his eightieth year, Siddhartha Gautama was walking through a park in autumn with a group of his loyal monks. The Enlightened One stopped to pick up a handful of dry leaves. "This is what I have said," the Buddha told his followers. Then he turned to the great expanse of leaves on the ground, stretching as far as the eye could see. "And this is what I have not said."

Was I waiting for a handful of dry leaves and missing the wisdom of the tree? I wondered. Was I being deceived by my own preconceptions, skipping over something else? I vowed to keep an open mind.

●

On day five, I was given the task of reading to the baby class before the assembly. The toddlers sat cross-legged in a row in the dirt while I read to them from a picture book called *The Tiger Who Came to Tea*. Each time I turned a page to reveal a new illustration, they squealed and cheered, calling out the animal names in English. "Tiger!" "Rabbit!" "Snake!" "Please, Uncle, read some more!" they begged when I finished the book, so I started in on *The Cat in the Hat*. With their age-old faces and tiny bodies, they couldn't have been more adorable. There were only two troublemakers, a pair of rambunctious boys at the rear of the group who were cutting up instead of listening. In the middle of my reading, from overhead, a woman's voice came booming down: "Boys in the back! Stop! Now!" I looked up and saw Mother Meera standing on the roof, one hand on her hip, a ferocious expression on her face. The boys lowered their heads and quieted down. Later that same day, one of these naughty boys started to misbehave again, during closing prayers. As if on cue, Mother Meera appeared out of nowhere, pinched the little hoodlum's ear, and led him out back for a talking-to.

•

That afternoon, we hired a driver to take us to the Rishi Valley School, seven miles up the road from Madanapalle. The school was founded in 1926 by Jiddu Krishnamurti (1895-1986), a remarkable sage known for his razor-sharp intellect and radical take on the spiritual life. K, as he liked to be called, was a native of Madanapalle and Mother Meera's opposite in temperament and teaching. Brilliant, vain, and obsessed with reason, K focused on ruthless inquiry and disregard for all forms of tradition. He was the blade to Mother Meera's chalice, penetrating, pointed, and severe. Yet K also shared qualities with Mother Meera. Like her, he recommended that followers exercise common sense and self-reliance. His famous dictum "The truth is a pathless land" shares with the Mother's way a rejection of rigid, formulaic practice or adherence to a single creed. Both warned against attachment to the teacher, confusing hero worship with divine connection, and against sacrificing personal freedom when choosing our path to God (a term K avoided). By the time I came to spiritual seeking, K had just died, but his books and video teachings soon became foundation stones of my spiritual life. I was eager to visit Rishi Valley and pay respect to this great teacher.

In the taxi on the way to the school, I noticed a dashboard ornament of the white-bearded, kerchief-headed Sai Baba of Shirdi, one of India's most popular saints. "Is that your guru?" I asked our driver, Raju.

"All holy people are guru," he said, meeting my eye in the rearview mirror. "Mother Meera is guru, too."

"No," I said. "At least she doesn't think so."

"Mother Meera saved my life," Raju continued, ignoring my objection. Then he proceeded to tell us his story. Raju had grown up on the street as one of those urchins in India who knock on the windows of stopped cars, begging for a few rupees. "When Mother first came here, I had no prospects. My friend brought me to her ashram for *darshan*. I sat down in front of her and there was so much love coming from her eyes!" Raju put his hand to his heart. "I began to have confidence after that," he went on. "Before Mother, no one loved me. She gave me good advice one day. She told me to find a job, any job, and stop this begging. She suggested that I should learn how to drive. That was seven years ago. Today, I have my own fleet of taxis. Other drivers work for me! Next month, I will be married. This is all because of Mother Meera."

"And your own hard work," I added. "Do you believe that Mother is divine?"

"The whole world is divine, no?" Raju answered. "The mahatmas like Mother, Sai Baba, K, they come to earth to remind us."

Raju pulled off the highway and left us at the entrance to the Rishi Valley School. David and I walked around for an hour, touring the bucolic campus, hundreds of acres of farmland dotted with freestanding buildings, groves of eucalyptus trees, vegetable gardens, and rain-fed streams. In the eucalyptus grove where K used to give his talks, we sat down to meditate in the shade. The air filled with the scent of menthol, the stillness interrupted by the occasional magpie screeching on a nearby branch. I imagined K as he would have appeared in those days, with his hooded, half-closed owl eyes, ramrod posture, and white-haired combover, speaking in his elegant Oxbridge tones about the "Immensity" (his term for God) and the great silence available to us outside our helmet of mental noise when we fully enter the present moment. Eloquent as K's spoken teachings were, it was his silence that had impressed me most, as it seemed to stream from his very being. The visceral power of his silent presence reminded me of Mother Meera's. K's biographer Mary Lutyens once described him as "the efflorescence of an age," and sitting there in the eucalyptus grove, I realized that the same could be said of Mother Meera, however different their bloom and hue. Both pointed to a new way of knowing God, beyond tribal religions and dogma. The eighteenth-century philosopher Louis-Claude de Saint-Martin believed that "all mystics speak the same language and come from the same country," and it was obvious to me as I thought of the two of them that Mother Meera and Krishnamurti did indeed share a longitude and latitude, however different their dialects or divergent the figures they cut in the world.

Back in the taxi, Raju offered to give us a tour of Mother Meera's other properties in Madanapalle. We stopped first at the farm site, where a grand retreat house was under construction, then at the Montessori school, where a few dozen well-behaved children waved at us from their classrooms. After that, Raju took us to a second, larger schoolhouse, where we were met by the woman who'd been leading the children in their chants before *darshan*. Plump and smiling in her peasant dress and sandals, Norina looked every inch the earth mother as she greeted us and led the way into the building, where classes had been canceled for the day. A German citizen of Egyptian heritage, with a girlish voice and infectious good humor, Norina explained that a hornets' nest in the neighbor's yard had yet to be removed, making it unsafe for the students. "Nothing happens on time in this country!" she chirped, shooing away a scary-looking monkey crouching on the wall behind us. She walked us up and down the halls and began to tell us about herself. A Coptic Christian who'd trained as a teacher, Norina had moved her life to Madanapalle three years earlier to run the school, at Mother Meera's request.

"At first, I wasn't happy!" Norina admitted. "I thought, 'No! I will be in India and Ma will be in Germany. I will never see her!' But Ma promised she was coming to India once a month, so I had to trust her." Norina opened the door to the nap room, the floor lined with mats where the children could sleep. "Now it is nice to see her," she said, "but I don't need to be with Ma to be *with* her, if you know what I mean. I don't need to live with her all the time in order to be happy." Norina closed the nap room door. "She brings so much joy into my life, you see. The kind of joy that is inside of myself. It doesn't depend on anything external. Not even Ma's physical presence."

Norina led us up to her private quarters. There were a half dozen photographs of Mother Meera hanging on the walls, unlike any images I'd seen before, taken with Norina's iPhone in airport lounges and other private spaces. The pictures showed another side of Mother Meera, the jolly, unguarded, gal-pal side. Norina giggled. "Ma and I do FaceTime together. We laugh so much! It is only in India where Ma is so serious. Sometimes, I worry about her."

"Why?" I asked.

"Because she does not care enough for her body," she told us. "Ma ignores it too much of the time. But the body needs a little bit of attention, too. Even divine personalities suffer physically." Norina showed us a photo of a dozing Mother Meera. "You know, Ma hardly ever sleeps. Maybe two hours. She is always working, working, working. No human being could do what she does! She doesn't like to eat much, either. Whenever I prepare special dishes for her, she pretends to enjoy, but I know she is only doing so for me. Ma always says, 'I'm not an eater.' The truth is, she forgets that she has a body. But she and I have so much fun! Ma makes very good jokes, you know."

"What kinds of jokes?"

"Ma loves to tease. But she's never unkind. For example, I always buy too much of everything," Norina said. "So when someone asks Ma where they can get something, she tells them, 'You can go to Norina. She buys one and gets ten free.' Or when I show her something really practical and cheap, she asks me if I bought a hundred!" Norina rolled her eyes. "Or when devotees ask her what special foods they should eat to be *spiritual*—special organic things or whatnot—Ma will tell them that people who shop at cheap supermarkets live longer."

Norina led us back downstairs to her office. "Ma's so down-to-earth," she said, plopping into a chair. "Whenever people come to her, all puffed up with spiritual ideas, Ma always goes *poomf!*" She gestured as if popping a balloon. "That's what she did with me. Before I came to Ma, I thought I was *holy*. I thought I was only *good*. Well, Ma took care of that right away! She showed me the other side of who I was, the arrogance, the vanity, the self-pity. The anger!" Norina admitted. "When these feelings used to come up in me, I really did not know what to do. I went to Ma and asked her. She said, 'In everyone's life, there has to be balance. If you have a happy time, then the sad time will soon be coming. If you always want sunshine, then you will not be happy.' Ma told me this because she knew it was my nature to always want sunshine. I wanted to be closer to God. What I thought of as God. So, of course, Ma brought me rain. How else could I grow? She knew that I needed to accept both."

Norina walked us back to Raju's taxi. "The same goes for our relationship to her. Ma wants us to love her also in all aspects. Not only to love her when she's sweet and nice."

I felt secretly guilty when Norina made this point.

"That is not love," she said.

Back at the ashram school, I continued to observe Mother Meera from a distance, remembering Norina's words. As she worked at her daily tasks, I noticed how weary she looked and how slowly she moved from job to job, as if plowing through a muddy field. On the morning of day six, I heard Mother reprimand Hilda for the children's lack of discipline during recess, prompting the poor woman to rush off in tears. That afternoon, there were mistakes with some project or other, and I watched in amazement as Mother's temper flared at the precise moment when one of the teachers was kneeling down to kiss her feet.

Among the volunteers, there were whispers about the daunting challenges of running the schools to Mother Meera's specifications. Her extreme frugality was one of the hurdles. Apparently, a staff member had asked permission to spend ten extra dollars a month on better Internet service and been told no. ("That money could feed two children a month," Mother had reminded him.) Explaining my clerical duties, Mohan specified that I should type using extra-narrow margins, since Mother doesn't like to waste paper. Her thrift seemed to be more problematic when it came to important administrative decisions. Hiring a professional full-time principal for the school would save a great many headaches, for instance. But this isn't how Mother Meera does things. When she wants a new house, she builds it herself. If something needs fixing, she figures it out. She packs her own suitcase, irons her own saris, and even, I was surprised to learn, now does much of her own bookkeeping, having hired and fired a few bad accountants. When devotees who know these jobs better than she does make such suggestions at the school, their ideas often fall on deaf ears.

Mother Meera is equally impervious to the human dramas that proliferate in her presence. As Adilakshmi reminded me, physical proximity to the divine often brings out the worst in people. Spiritual communities are, after all, microcosms of the larger world, populated by all sorts of characters, from the wise, cooperative, and tolerant to the pious, obnoxious, backbiting, and crazy. The community around Mother is especially diverse, with individuals running the gamut of religions, economic classes, professional sectors, sexual orientations, and political affinities.

During our visit, this particular group of volunteers ranged in age from twenty-two to seventy-eight and included a German plumber, an Italian designer, a Danish athlete and his father, two schoolteachers (Belgian and Indian), a dancer from Boston, a Malagasy entrepreneur, a well-dressed therapist from Toulouse, and a couple of English pensioners. The disagreements, gossip, and awkward dynamics were frequently in evidence. One of the volunteers was especially caustic and cornered me in the courtyard one morning before anyone else was awake. "I can't stand these bigots," he whispered. "You know, the ones who say Mother Meera is the only one. Or the best one. She never encourages this kind of thing!" The fellow looked around to make sure no one was listening. "I'm not interested in dogma or beliefs," he said. "That is what I love about Mother. She doesn't care about that kind of power. She knows she's not the only one! But the people around her?" He bugged his eyes and twirled a finger next to his temple. "Completely bananas, some of them. And bigots!" He seemed quite unaware of how biased he sounded himself.

Mother Meera doesn't mind such dissent. "God didn't make imperfect people. He made normal ones," she often says. In more than forty years of offering *darshan*, she has never refused anyone her blessing, explaining that this is the divine way. Asked if she would give *darshan* to Adolf Hitler or Saddam Hussein, Mother Meera says she would. To most of us, this extreme lack of prejudice is incomprehensible, yet it appears to be normal in the eyes of the divine. Enlightened individuals harbor no illusions about the abysmal aspects of human nature. To me, this is the most glaring difference between Mother Meera and an ordinary person, the most visible "proof" of her divinity: a preternatural tolerance of human failings and the ability to see behind people's masks to the souls hiding underneath, no matter how monstrous these masks might be. Meher Baba, who shared this divine perspective, referred to his most troubled followers as "broken furniture." This capacity for godly love, or agape, appears to be possible only among those rarefied sages who are not themselves broken and require nothing from those around them. Anandamayi Ma (1896-1982), a beloved avatar of the Divine Mother, described this sacred relationship in a photo book called *Matri Darshan*. "A saint is like a tree," she once said.

> She does not call anyone, neither does she send them away. She gives shelter to whoever cares to come, be it a man, woman, child, or an animal. If you sit under a tree

it will protect you from the weather, the scorching sun as well as from the pouring rain, and it will give you flowers and fruit. Whether a human being enjoys them or a bird tastes of them matters little to the tree; its produce is there for anyone who comes and takes it.

Requiring no reciprocity, divine representatives feel no need to divvy up their fruits like the rest of us, trapped in our patterns of tit-for-tat. Their gifts are offered selflessly to whoever might need them, regardless of their failings. "I want you to be completely yourself," Mother Meera has said. "Come to me exactly as you are. Everyone grows in a different way. Everyone has different needs. And everyone is unique for me. My love is equal for all."

Mother confirmed this to a devotee who, like me, was having her doubts. "One day, I screwed up my nerve to talk to Mother," this lady told me. "I had a lot of trauma in my family background and said, 'Mother, I'm so closed down. I need your help so I can actually feel love. I don't think anything but divine grace will help me.' She said, 'Okay.' Then I asked, 'Mother, do you ever hug people?' She smiled and said, 'Not so much.' The truth is that I'd seen her hug people a couple of times over the years, and it made me so mad and upset, even though I knew it was silly and immature. Anyway, the next thing I knew, Mother just gave me this huge hug. Not a little-touch kind of thing but a real hug. I was stunned. When it was over, I said, 'Mother, I love you so much I don't even know what to say.' 'Do you really think-I don't know that?'" she answered.

●

On the day Mother Meera left India to return to Germany, we'd eaten dinner in the town center and made our way back to the school, along the dung-strewn, dusty streets, past Brahma bulls tethered to washing machines, grazing on garbage, past yellow rickshaws swarming the intersections like bees, and shopkeepers chatting in storefront doorways. Beyond the Colony Gate, we walked by the Catholic retreat center, with its glassed-in, dark-skinned Virgin Mary, then on to the Shiva temple, with its twenty-foot, Pepto-Bismol-colored statue of the god flanked by his car-sized bull Nandi, and around the corner to Paramatman Way.

Mother Meera was sitting on the porch, sur-rounded by a group of ashram kids. These disadvan-taged children were her original inspiration for starting the school, a group of orphans without families to sup-port them, whom Mother Meera invited to live in her private home. A brain-damaged boy with a crooked leg was making whooping sounds and laughing, spin-ning in circles around Mother, while a mob of little girls stroked her hair and her sari, as others sat ador-ingly at her feet. Mother Meera seemed entirely at ease with the children. Instantly, I was consumed by envy. The ashram kids weren't prodding her with bor-ing questions or feeble esoteric inquiries. They wanted nothing from Mother but her love, a little attention, a word of kindness. By contrast, I was exploding with questions and overflowing with neediness. What had it been like for her, being an incarnation inside a child's body? How had she managed her little-girl feelings, and how had these emotional beginnings translated—or not—to Mother Meera? Was Kamala still inside her somewhere, or had she simply disappeared? Perhaps I would never know.

Mother Meera had continued to keep her distance, so all of my questions had gone unanswered. I'd struggled not to take this personally but mostly failed. Whatever lessons she might be sending me with her silence remained unclear. I'd had personal insights since arriving, but had they been intended by her? I was far from certain. When news had reached me in the morning that Mother was leaving that night, I'd been devastated. My window of opportunity was almost closed, and I was the last to know. As one last Hail Mary pass, I'd decided to send her a message, in the hope that she would change her mind. The note was imploring but polite, thanking Mother for letting us stay at the school and regretting *very much* that we hadn't spent any time together. I'd given the note to Mohan to pass along to Mother during their morning meeting, and had waited on tenterhooks for her reply. When Mohan returned after lunch, he'd handed me the unopened envelope and told me that Mother would not take it.

"Wouldn't take it?"

"She handed it back."

I wanted to pound the desk but didn't. There was now nothing more that I could do. Hidden in the shadows, watching the children as they played with Mother,

I felt like a genuine outcast. I went to our room and moped for an hour. At nine o'clock, Maurice invited the volunteers downstairs to say our goodbyes. We stood in the driveway, the fifteen of us, and after a few minutes, Mother emerged, followed by a helper carrying her suitcase. Maurice opened the car door so that she could slip into the passenger seat. As the car pulled away, Mother turned her face and grinned at us through the window, looking happier than she had all week. I didn't manage to catch her eye.

The following morning, before David and I left for Pondicherry, I found Adilakshmi to say goodbye. She was back at her desk, reading the paper. Adilakshmi asked how my time at the school had been, and I told her honestly what had happened. "You must learn to trust," she repeated, folding the paper in half.

I assured Adilakshmi that I was trying.

"Then you will see how the Mother works."

# 8

# THE DIVINE LIFE

Though Mother Meera has never had a living mentor, she does share a spiritual heritage with the sages of Pondicherry, Sri Aurobindo and Sweet Mother. This mystic couple has been a part of her life since Kamala's first visit to their tomb when she was thirteen. Mr. Reddy believed Mother Meera to be the Mother of the Future Transformation prophesied by Aurobindo, the avatar who would carry on the work of earthly divinization begun by Sweet Mother and himself.

To appreciate Mother Meera's place in our contemporary landscape, it helps to have an understanding of Aurobindo's unique spiritual vision. Integral Yoga is a radical synthesis of ancient wisdom and futuristic teachings unlike anything that preceded it. Before Aurobindo came along, religious traditions had concerned themselves almost exclusively with spiritual *ascent*, portraying the physical body as a barrier to awakening and its transcendence, or mortification, as a necessary step toward liberation. Aurobindo rejected this patriarchal, body-negative version of divinity and focused instead on reopening the door to the feminine principle, balancing the terrestrial (Shakti) and the divine (Shiva) into a blend of material and transcendental reality. Aurobindo countered traditional beliefs dating back three millennia to the Bhagavad Gita and believed the time had come for a new understanding of God. He suggested that spiritual *descent* could "transform human life into a Divine life on earth without the renunciation of the world." In other words, the age of the Father God was over.

Integral Yoga is based on three main principles. First, the Divine Mother, in whatever form she is honored, must be returned to her rightful place at the center of global spirituality if we hope to survive as a species. Second, the human race is a work in progress, an evolving stage on the continuum from material to divine existence. In the words of Aurobindo's contemporary, the Nobel Prize–winning philosopher Rudolf Eucken, "Man is the meeting-point of various stages of Reality." Finally, this divinization process depends on the entrance of a new spiritual Light into the material world for the first time in human history, as the quickening agent for this evolution. This last principle is the hardest for most of us to grasp.

In light of what we know today about energy science, the mind-body connection, electromagnetic fields, and the enlightening effects of spiritual practice on the brain, Aurobindo's vision of this future human does not seem completely implausible. Aurobindo put it this way in his book, *The Life Divine*: "Our current status of evolution is still an intermediary stage of being on its way to the unfolding of spirit, and the self-revelation of Divinity in all things." He then explained the crucial role of the Mother in this evolutionary process.

The universe was created by a God that has both masculine and feminine aspects. The masculine divine is beyond all understanding. The feminine divine manifests itself as the physical universe and as the intelligent power that moves the universe. All created things, whether human being or planet earth, span a spectrum of realities from the lowest, the material, to the highest, pure light and spiritual energy. The entire universe is evolving, as the divine introduces progressively more Light into the material world in a way that will lead in the end to its transubstantiation.

This Light-powered path to divine connection mirrors with surprising accuracy Mother Meera's description of how the Light works. Also, her visionary experiences with Aurobindo when she was still Kamala Reddy suggest a kind of passing of the torch. She described this transfer of spiritual power in Adilakshmi's book, *The Mother*:

> Once, Sweet Mother gave me a rose. I took the flower to Sri Aurobindo's *samadhi* [tomb]. I knew it was not an ordinary flower. It was my soul. I held onto it fiercely. But as I was walking, Sri Aurobindo snatched it from me without my knowing. I was very sad because I had lost my soul. Then Sri Aurobindo called me and asked me why I was so sad. I told him that I had lost my soul. He said, "Your soul is not lost and

could never be," and then he showed me the flower he had stolen. Then he replaced Sweet Mother's rose with a golden rose and told me that this golden rose was his soul and that it would stay with me always.

●

I traveled to Pondicherry to visit Aurobindo's tomb in the hope of understanding this sacred connection. Pondicherry is a postcard-pretty town with wide, clean streets and whitewashed houses streaming with ribbons of bougainvillea. Before dawn, the beachside promenade is crowded with joggers and exercise buffs doing their calisthenics in the sand. Gabbing women in saris and shalwar kameez power walk in tennis shoes past espresso bars and terraced restaurants and the fourteen-foot statue of Mahatma Gandhi holding his staff. Vendors sell lotus blossoms from tin tubs at roadside stands, purple, white, and pink, and there are tchotchkes and photographs everywhere commemorating the town's patron saints. Ten minutes from the gate of the Sri Aurobindo Ashram is the modest white bungalow at 22 rue St. Honoré where Kamala stayed with Mr. Reddy on her first visit.

We left our sandals outside the ashram gate and made our way to the shaded courtyard, where two dozen pilgrims had come to pay their respects at the shared tomb. The silence was echoing and profound. We waited on line for our turn to touch the white marble tombstone itself. Beneath the porticoes and the great ash tree at the center of the courtyard, visitors sat with their eyes closed or gazed peacefully into the garden. The tomb was blanketed with flowers—marigolds, lotuses, jasmine, tulasi—a sheath of fragrant, brilliantly hued petals covering its length from head to foot. As we waited our turn, a stooped old Indian woman with vitiligo performed an elaborate ritual in front of us, dipping her fingers in holy water first, then sprinkling it over herself four times, touching flowers with the backs and fronts of her blotchy hands, left then right, and scraping her fingertips through her white hair. A well-coiffed Pakistani businesswoman in a pantsuit and pearls prayed with her palms joined in front of her heart, and a teenage boy knelt beside her, pressing his forehead against the marble, his lips moving fast as he whispered to God.

We sat in the shade to meditate. I imagined Mother Meera as she must have looked on the day she first visited the tomb, poised and beautiful, dressed in the new silk sari bought by Mr. Reddy for this special occasion. I pictured the scene of her standing there, closing her eyes, and disappearing into an altered state. No one present had any idea of what was going on inside her. The familiar questions rushed into my mind. Does she still have such extreme experiences? What is it like to be free of the body while being inside one? Would the world be divinized as Aurobindo had predicted? These riddles bounced around in my mind like soap bubbles outside a bolted door. I was standing before that door, wanting in, hungering to know the truth, to understand what being an avatar means, to be let in on this divine secret. But the door wouldn't budge.

I read Aurobindo's explanation of how divine incarnation works, and about the nature of the avatar. Strangely, the more I read about avatarhood, the less like science fiction it sounded. Aurobindo acknowledged the challenge posed by the avatar to our consensus reality. "The Avatar is one of the most difficult [concepts for the Western mind] to accept or to understand of all the ideas streaming in from the East upon the rationalized human consciousness," he admitted.

> It is apt to take it at best for a mere figure for some high manifestation of human power, character, genius, great work done for the world... and at worst to regard it as a superstition. The materialist, necessarily, cannot even look at it, since he does not believe in God ... to the thoroughgoing dualist who sees an unbridgeable gulf between the human and the divine nature, it sounds like blasphemy.
>
> [And yet] the idea of the Avatar ... comes in naturally as a perfectly rational and logical conception. For all here is God, is the Spirit or Self-existence.... Far from the Infinite being unable to take on finiteness, the whole universe is nothing else but that.... Far from the Spirit being incapable of form or matter or mind and assuming a limited nature or a body, all here is nothing but that, the world exists only by that connection, that assumption.

I stopped reading for a moment, struck by one particular sentence. *Far from the Infinite being unable to take on finiteness, the whole universe is nothing else but that.* I could not deny how true this rang. Was it possible that the doubt over divine incarnation was founded on a misguided assumption? A false belief in the unbridgeable gulf between the human and the divine? What if this dualistic conjecture was completely false and there was nothing in this world *but* God, as Aurobindo was saying? The implications of this were revelatory. If it were true that God exists not only within our reach but within *us*—as the very stuff we are made of—then original sin goes right out the window. All the Puritan propaganda about the sinfulness of the body would suddenly become obsolete.

Putting the avatar question in plain language dissolved this imaginary divide, making divinity—the potential to embody godliness—more relatable as part of the human condition. Assuming that all of creation is nothing but a spectrum of consciousness, it no longer seemed quite so far-fetched to believe that avatars—higher forms of sentient beings—might be moving among us, just as other forms of genius mutate into human populations. As a Mozart is born hearing music he never learned, self-described divine incarnations like Mother Meera might well be born fully cognizant—if that's the right word—of the divinity we all share.

•

There were references to such spiritual geniuses in every tradition I encountered. Buddhists call them *Tathagata*.

Some Islamic sects describe them as *Nur*. Members of the Baha'i faith refer to avatars as Manifestations of God, and in Kabbalistic Judaism the term for such holy beings is *tzaddik*. In Christianity, of course, the avatar not only exists but is the central figure of the religion: Christ's descent as God's only Son. Unlike these other faiths, however, Christians believe that there can be only one Messiah and that His name is Jesus Christ. Unfortunately, this divine exclusivity has caused terrible cruelty to be carried out in the name of God. In *The Perennial Philosophy*, Aldous Huxley articulated this crucial point. "Because Christians believed that there had only been one Avatar, Christian history has been disgraced by more and bloodier crusades, interdenominational wars, and proselytizing imperialism than has the history of Hinduism and Buddhism," Huxley wrote. Fundamentalist aggression of any kind is contrary to the way of the Mother, of course.

Apparently, a vast difference exists between avatars and even the most accomplished gurus. Gurus perfect themselves over time, working through their human karma. Avatars are believed to be karma-free. When Mother Meera says that she has "never been born as a human being," I believe that's what she means. As she has explained in *Answers, Part I*, "Avatars have no good or bad karma. Karma is only for human beings." Neither does the term "enlightenment" apply to individuals like her, she tells us. "Enlightenment is only for human beings. Avatars are born with enlightenment." Human gurus and spiritual masters struggle up toward God through intensive practice, while the avatar works her or his way down from God consciousness in order to serve humanity. That is why the avatar's ability to help others is so much greater than a guru's, according to Eastern thought. The nineteenth-century saint Ramakrishna, himself a devotee of the Divine Mother, compared gurus to ferryboats capable of carrying a few souls across the sea to liberation, whereas avatars are more like ocean liners, able to deliver millions of souls to the enlightened state.

Different avatars describe their identity in undeniably similar language. Consider the statements of Anandamayi Ma, Meher Baba, and Mother Meera on the subject of who exactly they are.

ANANDAMAYI MA:
Father, there is little to tell. My consciousness has never associated itself with this temporary body. Before I came on this earth, Father, I was the same. As a little girl, I was the same. I grew into woman-hood, but still I was the same. When the family in which I had been born made arrangements to have this body married, I was the same.... And, Father, in front of you now, I am the same. Ever afterward, though the dance of creation changes around me in the hall of eternity, I shall be the same.

MEHER BABA:
The avatar appears in different forms, under different names, at different times, in different parts of the world. As his appearance always coincides with the spiritual birth of man, so the period immediately preceding his manifestation is always one in which humanity suffers from the pangs of the approaching birth. In this form of flesh and blood, I am that same Ancient One. I am

God. I am in you all. I never come and I never go. I am present everywhere.

M O T H E R   M E E R A :
Each Avatar can be considered as one facet of a diamond, and at the same time the whole diamond. My body changes and your perception of me changes as you grow in knowledge. I have always been the same and will always be the same. What you see is one facet, but the whole diamond is behind it and around it. I do what Paramatman tells me. If he tells me to come down, I come down.

Each incarnation is said to be born with a unique spiritual mission. In Mother Meera's case, this mission is to bring down a particular Light that changes human history. "The Light has never been used before," she says. "Like electricity, it is everywhere, but one must know how to activate it. I have come for that." According to her, there are several other incarnations of the Divine Mother alive today, each embodying a different face of the supreme feminine. Mother likens her own personality to that of the goddess Durga, a more patient aspect of the Divine Mother who loves her children more and punishes less.

Mother Meera also claims to be in contact with her other Divine cohorts. Some of these avatars, including the hugging saint Ammachi, are well known to the public. Others do their divine work in private, apparently. Among these avatars is a mysterious woman whom Mother Meera calls Loka Shakti Shanti (Mother of World Peace). Aside from the fact that she was born in 1978, nothing more is known about Loka Shakti Shanti, whom Mother Meera says she will meet once or twice in her lifetime, but whose identity Mother will not divulge. In fact, Mother is strictly reticent when it comes to commenting on the divinity of other spiritual figures. She seems to understand that such labeling easily becomes a parlor game of who's an avatar and who is not among devotees of various masters competing for spiritual status. Mother recommends that we judge our teachers by what we feel in our own hearts, leaving divine categorization to those with eyes to perceive such differences.

Ocean-liner avatars do appear to share one visible distinction from ferryboat gurus, however: preternatural stamina that defies logical explanation. Ammachi, for example, commonly gives *darshan* to tens of thousands of people at a time, without a break, taking each visitor into her arms and emerging unfatigued and smiling from these marathon gatherings, her white sari sopping wet from those who have wept on her shoulder. Though frail and sick toward the end of his life, Meher Baba offered *darshan* to thousands of devotees in a day, as well, touching the head of each one without visible signs of weakness. There are similar reports concerning Sai Baba of Shirdi and his modern counterpart, Sathya Sai Baba. Mother Meera confided to me that she could offer *darshan* to an unlimited number of people at a gathering but keeps her sessions to ninety minutes since "Westerners cannot sit that long." Asked by a worried devotee about the demands of a relentless schedule that often takes her to three continents in a single month, Mother Meera was typically unfazed. "If the whole world came to me, my work would not be interrupted or deflected for a moment," she told him. "Nothing can and nothing will interfere with my work. I am working on all planes. Everywhere. How could anything disturb my work?"

This is not to say that avatars don't experience the pain of the body; they're simply not affected by pain the same way as the rest of us are. When Kamala's foot was punctured through by a giant thistle, she screamed as any little girl would and clung to her father's neck as he carried her to the next village to see the doctor. When Mother Meera underwent a nose operation in 1986, the pain was so excruciating that she passed out, Adilakshmi reports; still, Mother continued to bless devotees from her hospital bed, explaining that "this is the Divine way... every minute is used." According to Mother Meera, the pain experienced by avatars "is not felt so deeply" or experienced as suffering. Nevertheless, the divine incarnation "has a dharma [role] like everybody else and must bear the pain of being an Avatar."

Mother has a similar response to emotional pain. Though subject to unpleasant feelings, she seems to pay them little attention. When asked if she is ever hurt when devotees treat her badly, Mother replies that she tends to take it lightly, though "on very rare occasions it is painful." The most challenging period of her life came after Mr. Reddy's death, when Mother seemed overwhelmed by sorrow. Daniel described finding her in the stairwell one day with tears streaming down her face. Mother touched her heart and said, "*Schmerz*"—pain. In the book *Answers*, she points out that while devotees have the opportunity to offer their pain to Mother Meera, she cannot offer her own pain to anybody but God. From a human perspective, this sounds terribly lonely, but for those in direct communication with the divine, loneliness does not seem to exist. This is not to say that Mother is immune to the presence of those around her. "Through the love of those who come to me, I can bear it," she says of human pain. "If there is love and sincerity and devotion, I will live longer. It is the same for every Avatar."

•

Another paradox of the avatar's life is the general public's lack of interest in their very existence. This relative absence of recognition during their lifetime appears to come with the job. As Jesus says in Luke 4:24, "No man is a prophet in his own country." Meher Baba described this general ambivalence in an interview with an English journalist in 1954. "When I say I am the Avatar," he spelled out on the alphabet board he used during his decades-long silence, "there are few who feel happy, some who feel shocked, and many who take me for a hypocrite, a fraud, a supreme egoist, or just mad." This antipathy is more pronounced in the West. According to Mother Meera, Westerners give excessive importance to the materialistic worldview, and it is for this reason that most people have little desire to consider the possibility of divine incarnation. "Even when the Avatar comes, many Westerners are not willing to give the time to meet him or her," she explains in *Answers, Part 1*.

This last point raises a common question: Why do so many saints and sages hail from the East and particularly from India? An obvious explanation would be the Eastern receptivity to the phenomenon of enlightenment itself. For millennia, the cultures of the Orient have cultivated belief systems, rituals, and languages whose main focus is spiritual life. If you thumb through a Sanskrit dictionary, you'll find many hundreds of terms for describing the different dimensions of human consciousness. Try the same thing with a Western-language dictionary and you'll come across a paltry handful. "English is impoverished just where Sanskrit is richest: in terms that succinctly describe finely nuanced levels of expanded awareness and the realities such states reveal," writes the Vedic scholar Alistair Shearer in his translation of the Upanishads.

In the absence of language for describing metaphysical states, it becomes easier to imagine that they don't exist. Had Kamala Reddy been born an American child experiencing visions and altered states, she would most likely have been medicated and placed in psychiatric care. There's a long history in the West of punishing or misdiagnosing people given to nonordinary states of consciousness. In the absence of language or a cultural context for describing these states, we easily miss what's under our noses. For an article about homelessness, I once traveled around the United States talking with people who lived on the street. In the course of my research, I came across an old man who was clearly in an enlightened state but had been diagnosed as schizophrenic and rejected by society. "God is like the air," he told me, his wrinkled face radiant and serene. This filthy, unkempt squatter had eyes brimming over with love and a presence that was quite transcendental. In India, he would be revered as a *sadhu* (renunciant) worthy of alms and respect. In America, he's just a crazy, homeless beggar.

With their emphasis on sin and the need for redemption, organized Western religions, for all their strengths, offer very little hope of spiritual liberation as a human possibility (except in heaven, if you're lucky). This materialistic view runs directly counter to Eastern understanding, where liberation is viewed as the very reason for our existence. In Mother Meera's case, the good fortune of an Indian childhood permitted her spiritual nature to flower without restraint. As Martin Goodman explains in his memoir about Mother Meera,

> Her upbringing up till age eleven offered nothing to deny her perception of her own divinity. There was no school education designed to mold her into the ways of society, no media to invade her thoughts with its opinions and fantasies, no belief system that suggested gods do not roam the earth in human form and play out their dramas above Indian fields. On the contrary, the belief system in her village assured her that such divine play is the natural condition of the world.

The purpose of the divine appearing in these concentrated, brilliant forms is to remind us of what is possible in a human body. We go to *darshan* not for some otherworldly experience but to meet the enlightened parts of ourselves. The purpose of a spiritual master is to reflect back the power that we, too, possess, to enkindle the spark of eternal flame burning in us at every moment. That is the meaning of the mystic call, "the innate tendency of the human spirit towards complete harmony with the transcendental order," as Evelyn Underhill defines it. "Mysticism" is a misconstrued term too often confused with fantasy, magic, and New Age nonsense. Yet our inbuilt mystic faculty is no more fantastical than the gift for being transported by music, elevated by a gorgeous sunset, or carried beyond ourselves by the startling power of love.

Everyone is a closet mystic, though we're mostly too preoccupied by everyday life to acknowledge it. Speaking for the majority, the contemporary theologian Frederick Buechner puts it this way:

> We are all of us more mystics than we believe or choose to believe. Life is complicated enough as it is, after all. Through some moment of beauty or pain, some sudden turning in our lives, we catch glimmers at least of what the saints are blinded by; only then, unlike the saints, we tend to go on as though nothing has happened. To go on as though something has happened, even though we are not sure what it was or just where we are supposed to go with it, is to enter the dimension of life that religion is a word for.

The least religious among us have glimpses of this mystic state on a regular basis, though we fail to recognize their source. Walking in nature, making love, or gazing up at the naked sky, you suddenly become aware of a window opening up inside you, providing entrée to an unseen dimension beyond the senses. Words like "awe," "wonder," "rapture," and "epiphany" point to this mystic expansion; so do transformational states of profound trauma, loss, or grief. There's a strange account of a grief-stricken disciple relating a tragic story about her life to Anandamayi Ma. Suddenly the saint began to laugh uncontrollably, until tears rolled down her cheeks. The woman was shocked by this response and asked Anandamayi Ma why she would laugh at her misery. "Because you are being shown the end of misery through the cracks that this misery is opening in your heart," the holy woman told her. "Through them you can see the sun of the Self shining."

According to the ancient scriptures, this Self—the source of mystic awareness—is accessible to us at all times through genuine spiritual practice. Since the ultimate reality (God) does not change, we require access to an unchanging awareness in order to perceive it. This is the purpose of meditation, yoga, self-inquiry, and all forms of prayer: they cultivate this unchanging awareness. Four thousand years before Sigmund Freud or the fMRI machine, which can measure the effects of meditation on the brain, the sages of the Upanishads discovered that this awareness is the very foundation of our existence. Our consciousness is made up of four primary levels, according to the ancient teachings, each with its own unique physiological changes that provide a different experience of what we call reality.

The first three levels—waking, sleeping, and dreaming—are well known to everyone. We spend our lives passing among these states without giving it a second thought. Underlying these three states and obscured by them, however, is a hidden substratum of constant awareness, referred to simply as the fourth. This awareness is transcendental—beyond time, space, and causation—and is the essence of who we are. "When the fourth is lived continuously alongside the other three states coming and going as before, there is enlightenment," according to the Isha Upanishad. This is not just a mood of feeling good in the waking state but an entirely different level of consciousness, with its own physiology and its own reality. It is said that the fourth is as different from waking as waking is from dreaming. "When the conceptual veil through which we ordinarily see the world is lifted, each limited object shines with the boundless Light of the spirit, and each transitory experience is a celebration of eternity."

Mystic experience tends to happen when we least expect it. I learned this on that first trip to India, a few months after meeting Mother Meera. Andrew and I were staying in a beachside hotel in Mahabalipuram, two hours' drive north of Pondicherry. Every evening just after sunset we would stroll along the beach into town. One day, we set out as usual along the sand in the direction of the nearby Shiva temple. It was an especially colorful twilight, with an opalescent sky and the largest moon I'd ever seen, the color of yellow pearl, hanging so low it nearly touched the horizon. The moment was too beautiful not to savor, so we sat down to meditate at the water's edge.

I watched the moon for several minutes, then finally closed my eyes. When I did so, the face of Mother Meera appeared across my inner vision—holographically, in three dimensions, just as if she were there—then seemed to converge with the glow of the moon. I became aware that I was leaning forward as if about to receive her *darshan*; then I laid my hands on the wet sand, palms down, and at that precise moment a wave broke, sending a shudder through the ground and directly into my body. The wave's vibration, the sound of the surf, and Mother's Meera's glowing face all seemed to coalesce with the moonlight. I felt shaken awake all of a sudden, electrified by the world around me.

When I opened my eyes, I was aware of being in an altered state. It wasn't hallucinatory, exactly, more an intensification of seeing accompanied by a weird sort of omnipresence. My perceptional field was higher, deeper; the sky, the moon, the tumbling surf, my fingertips touching the sand, all were pulsating softly together. I was seeing more than the surface of objects, which no longer seemed to be separate things. I had the strong impression of *knowing* them, feeling the scenery inside my skin. I stood and walked up to my knees in the water; Andrew was shouting from somewhere behind me. I felt my body turn slowly in his direction but when Andrew asked me to describe how I felt, a verbal response seemed beside the point. As we strolled together toward the temple, I was conscious of being inside my own skin while watching it from the outside as well.

There was nothing dramatic in any of this; the experience was extremely subtle. I could feel things, viscerally, without using my hands, simply by looking softly enough. I sensed that my breath had changed, too, as if I were being breathed by my surroundings. The palm trees, the ocean, the moon, my friend: we were all being breathed by that same spirit, held in the web that connected our bodies. It felt as though if I moved my arm, I could touch the branch of that tree in the distance. The breeze itself seemed sentient, alive. When we came to the end of the beach, Andrew and I turned toward town, ate our dinner, and made our way back to the hotel.

This altered state lasted until the next morning. Neither talking, eating, washing, nor sleeping interrupted its peaceful flow. When I drifted off to sleep, some part of me remained awake and watched myself as I rested. By sunrise, there was a pleasing afterglow, but the episode had ended. Nothing like this ever happened to me again.

In a poem, the Indian poet Rabindranath Tagore writes, "Beauty is simply reality seen with the eyes of love." For those few hours in Mahabalipuram, I had seen with the eyes of love, and the view had been extraordinary. Amazing, too, is the little-known fact that our bodies are wired for self-transcendence. Did you know that when you open your eyes after sleeping, the previous day's top layer of vision receptor cells are scorched away by the entering light, thus giving you, literally, new eyes? Or that the first sound you hear on waking vibrates away the prior day's auditory cells, meaning that when the cock crows, you hear it with physically new ears? Wonder is part of what makes us human. The body is full of signs and wonders only now being glimpsed through the lens of science.

We're changed cognitively by the presence of awe, in fact which points us to the eternal dimension. A member of the first American climbing team to scale Mount Everest described his own brush with the timeless present. Returning from the peak, Willi Unsoeld paused on a high pass to admire the transcendent view. As he turned around, he saw a small blue flower in the snow. "I don't know how to describe what happened," he told researchers Alice and Walden Howard. "Everything opened up and flowed together and made some kind of sense, and I was at complete peace. I have no idea how long I stood there. It could have been minutes or hours. Time melted. But when I came down, my life was different."

These blue-flower moments are passing us by every day but the workaday mind needs a shock or an epiphany to stop it in its habitual tracks. When this happens, our lives are never the same: we've glimpsed the world from outside the bubble. We've come face-to-face with what Mother Meera and her kind are reflecting back to us: a divine world just beyond our sight. A doorway to our own true nature. An invitation to back where we came from.

# 9

## THE LOVERS

A few months after leaving Madanapalle, I flew to Germany and stayed at Darshan Hall, a manor house acquired by the Mother Meera Foundation in the winter of 1991. Darshan Hall is a vast château situated on a mountainside in the Rhineland below Schloss Schaumburg, a twelfth-century castle straight out of the Brothers Grimm. The ninety-room mansion has the hushed, sterile air of a mystic sanatorium and serves as a retreat center for devotees from around the world. The scale of the building surprised me at first; it's a far cry from the working-class home in Thalheim where Mother still lives, a few miles down the road. After two days at the manor, I was finally able to find my room without getting lost in the wrong hallway.

I'd come to Germany to interview some of Mother Meera's closest disciples. I was eager to know how their spiritual lives had been affected over a period of many years by exposure to the Paramatman Light. I hoped that they would be able to tell me how Mother Meera's presence had changed them, including their relationship to God. What had been the boons and conflicts of spending decades in her proximity? What had they seen in Mother's most private moments that offered insight into the avatar's life and its effects on the people around them?

I began by speaking to Terry, a retired IT specialist from Holland who spends more time with Mother. Meera these days than anyone else in her inner circle. Affable, low-key, and easy to be with, Terry is Mother's ideal travel companion and majordomo, an orderly, bright-eyed, unflappable guy whose sunny disposition stands out in her entourage of moody Germans and Slavs.

"She's been more like a good friend from the very beginning," Terry began when we met in my kitchen for a cup of tea. At seventy-three, Terry looks twenty years younger, with his youthful smile and full head of blond hair. "Mother has a very good sense of humor," he told me. "It matches mine very well. So our connection is quite informal. I relate to her very normally."

"Do you see her as a divine incarnation?"

"Let me put it to you this way," Terry replied, leaning forward and folding his hands on the table. "I see Mother almost all the time, in her normal, private life. I see how she behaves behind the scenes. How she treats people and acts in different situations. What I can tell you is that Mother is as totally different from a human being as one can possibly be."

"And yet you call her a friend?" I noted. Tony shrugged as if to say that both things are true. "There is not the lightest trace of ego," he assured me. "Putting herself first. Placing herself on a pedestal or thinking of herself instead of others. With Mother, there is only helping. Without any thought for herself. Only love."

"What about the Paramatman Light?"

Terry explained that for reasons unbeknownst to him, it took ten years before he experienced the Light. "I woke up in the middle of the night and had the sense that something was coming," he told me matter-of-factly. "Then this energy started to enter into me from the soles of my feet. It was colorless and cool and kept me up the whole night. It continued the whole next day, until it finally subsided." He took a sip of tea. "The next time I saw Mother, I asked her if it was the Paramatman Light. She said, 'Yes.' I asked her how she knew, and Mother said, 'I can see it.'"

I admitted to Terry how otherworldly this sounded. "Maybe, but this is what happened," he said. "Most spiritual teaching is like shoveling snow. But with Mother, it's like the sun comes up and melts the snow." I was struck by this lovely analogy. "This process went on for me for a couple of years, more or less frequently, in different events and in different forms. Sometimes it was so powerful, it felt like a storm was raging inside me. Other times, it was like my body was filled with gold dust. For a year or two, it was doing all these different things," Terry reported, describing *kriyas*, the physical shivers and shakes that sometimes accompany mystic experience. "I can tell you that it was pure grace," he assured me. "It was not something you can learn by yourself. It came from a different dimension. Then one week, nothing happened and I got kinda angry. I went to Mother and asked what to do. All she said is 'Experiences come and go.' It took some time for me to accept this. I was so attached to those experiences."

"So the Light didn't take away your negative feelings?"

"Certainly not," Terry assured me. "I can still get angry and have an emotional life. This is normal. The idea that you become like an angel after a spiritual awakening, speaking softly and pretending to be perfect..." He made a disgusted face. "It's not like that at all. But the Light did change me."

"Can you tell me how? Specifically?"

"It is difficult to say what it did under the surface," Terry admitted. "But I feel a certain lightness in me. In all the cells. Also, my attitude to spiritual practices has changed. I've realized that it is all grace—that you cannot *earn* it. My experiences have helped me let go of all the fixed rules about spiritual life that you read in books. You know, this is spirit, this is not spirit. That kind of thing. Now I can laugh at all that! It's all gone. Mother always says that every soul is an individual, and what works for one person may not be right for another. That's why spiritual rules don't work."

Terry checked his watch and prepared to go. "What makes it so special being with her, and working with her, is that when you see her eyes in private, they have that same Light shining all the time like they do in *darshan*. It's not like when she gives *darshan* she goes into some trance. She's always like that. When she looks at you, or smiles in the course of a day, well, it's like..." He stood up from his chair.

"Like what, Terry?"

He searched for the right words. "Like a hundred suns shining," he said.

•

Next I spoke again to Ulrich Reinhold. Ulrich is the

loose cannon in Mother's close circle, the one most likely to say anything to anybody, at any time, without self-consciousness or restraint. Ulrich oversees many of Mother's construction projects and isn't shy about letting you know how much he enjoys the sound of his own voice.

"I broke up with the love of my life two years ago," Ulrich began. "For three months, I was in Mother's living room every day, crying my eyes out of my head. Mother would be cleaning the toilet and I'd be sitting on her bed, crying. Mother would be doing office work and I'd be sitting there, crying. I'd never experienced anything like this. It was so embarrassing!" he told me. "You know what Mother told me? She said, 'Ulrich, you have no one else to open your heart to.'"

"That sounds like something a friend would say."

"She's the best friend you can have in the world," he agreed. "She just looks in your heart and sees what you need. I was in so much pain back then. I asked Mother if she could please change it. She said, 'Of course, I can change it easily. But that will not help you in the long term. I can help you go through these experiences. But I can't take the pain away from you. Otherwise, you wouldn't learn anything.'"

Before meeting Mother Meera, Ulrich had been an unhappy, highly successful private contractor in Frankfurt. "I was a millionaire and owned several companies," he explained. "But there was no happiness inside me. I was such an angry person. Nothing was working in my life. When things didn't go the way I wanted them to, I freaked out. I had no compassion for other people. Nothing."

"And Mother's power helped to change that?"

"Most definitely. Things have gotten better for me. But very slowly," Ulrich confessed. "I'm one of these dull idiots, you see. It takes me a long time to change. I once asked Mother, 'Why are there so many neurotic people around you?' She said that each of us represents a certain aspect of humanity and she is working on us. When I asked her why so much darkness comes up when we're around her, she told me, 'That's the only way to transform it.'"

I thought about my own dark feelings in India, which had hardly transformed since my return. "I think she is saying that if we are not able to live together in this house in harmony and joy," Ulrich continued, "then how can we expect the world to change?" Ulrich described Mother's own ability to harmonize with her environment. "When you see her shopping in the city, she is not running around with a beautiful sari. She's wearing her old jeans and a sweatshirt. But even though Mother is completely down-to-earth, she is also beyond anything."

"What do you mean by 'beyond'?" I asked.

"You feel her power, but you know you can't reach her. None of us can keep up with her pace. Twenty-two hours a day. It's impossible. And Mother remembers everything! She can tell me the exact measurements of some project or other by the millimeter, and I don't even have this information in my files."

Ulrich gave me another example of Mother's psychic acuity. One day, his special tool kit disappeared from the work site. He was certain that his tools were gone forever and reported the theft to Mother Meera. "She told me to look in the bathroom upstairs. I went there but I couldn't find them. Mother told me to look inside the washing machine. I opened it, and there they were! I asked Mother how she knew they were there. 'I just know,' she told me. 'When I need to know, I see it.'"

Like Norina and Terry, Ulrich shares plenty of laughs with Mother Meera. One afternoon, he and Mother were building an armoire together and accidentally got locked inside it. "We were crammed together," Ulrich remembered. "Face-to-face. I was so uncomfortable! But Mother was just laughing and laughing." On another occasion, he accidentally touched Mother Meera's hand while they were working together and had a sort of out-of-body climax. "It was pure bliss, I tell you," said Ulrich. "An orgasm of ten minutes is nothing compared to this! When I asked Mother if I could do it again, she said no." Ulrich laughed. "She is an absolutely untouchable person."

Then there was the incident with the *darshan* chair. Working in Darshan Hall, Ulrich inadvertently sat in Mother Meera's chair. He remembered the protest that ensued: "Everybody started to freak out! But when Mother saw me, all she said was 'Ulrich, please don't do it again. This is my chair. I don't want anyone sitting on it. If you want to do my job, you can apply for it. But I can tell you, it is not nice work!'"

Ulrich and I talked about how it must be for her, touching so much suffering—so intimately—every day of her life. "She is going to the very source of our pain," he said. "Down to the root. To whatever needs to be purified." He paused. "Suffering is a lonely experience—no one wants to go there with you. It's dark and smells down there. Like when I'm cleaning toilets here in the building because the pipes are blocked. No one wants to be there with me. There's only one person standing there beside me, and that's Mother. She's not afraid of anything."

●

Fearlessness has indeed been Mother Meera's most conspicuous trait since she was a young child. This intrepidness is nowhere more obvious than in Mother's decision to remain in Germany, even though she was a foreigner in a country so deeply traumatized by the Holocaust. According to Adilakshmi, Mother chose to live in Germany because of the two World Wars. ("The wound is here," she said.) At Darshan Hall, I spoke to a devotee whose parents had had Nazi affiliations in the Second World War but were deeply healed by Mother Meera's *darshan*.

"My father could be cruel," Elsa told me. "He was a parole officer in Munich with a drinking problem. Very often, he was totally irrational. My father terrified me. So I ran away as far as I could from my parents' house. I tried living in Portugal, where I pretended not to be German. I did everything possible to deny my heritage. But you can't run forever," Elsa confided.

"Eventually, when my parents were old and sick, I needed to come home. I stayed with them but got to *darshan* as often as possible. My father had no interest in spirituality at all. His heart was shut away for most of his life. But even he noticed how happy I was when I returned from Thalheim. He asked me to tell him about Mother Meera, which amazed me. When I talked to my father about the love I felt from Mother, he seemed to change. It was the first time he appeared gentle to me in all his life. When he finally died, my father was different from the man I knew before."

Elsa continued. "After that, my mother became very depressed. The doctor said, 'From now on, your mother will just lie in bed and stare at the ceiling.' I thought to myself, 'Well, if that is true, then she can do that at Mother Meera's house in Schaumburg!' I asked Mother if I could bring my own mother there, and she said yes. When we arrived, my mother looked over the valley and said that it reminded her of France, where she and my father had lived before the war. She'd loved it there. And you know what?" Elsa asked with a smile. "She never stayed in bed, the way the doctors said she would. Never! Even later, after I was forced to put her in an old-age home, the nurses would say to me, 'Ah, your mother is making jokes again.' Jokes? My mother? That was a first! Or she would be doing exercises in her bed. I could hardly believe the change in her. Sometimes, I'd come into the room and she would be absolutely bathed in bliss." Elsa's face brightened at the memory. "My mother died the following year. Her time near Mother Meera was the happiest I had ever seen her. It was an extraordinary blessing."

●

Some Jewish survivors have also experienced unexpected healings because Mother Meera is in Germany. A friend of mine, the performance artist Nina Wise, has a father who narrowly escaped arrest by the Gestapo. "I had mixed feelings about Germany, to say the least," she told me. Nina is a brilliant comedian with a sharp mind and a deadpan delivery. "A friend told me about Mother Meera," she said. "What I'd heard is that she pulls down light from the center of the universe and sends it into your body." She smiled as if to say "Really?" "Then she unties your karmic knots, whatever that means. Anyway, I was curious, but when my father found out I was going to Germany, he was very unhappy with me."

Nina had been raised to see Germany as verboten, yet despite her father's anger, she traveled to Thalheim at the invitation of a trusted friend. "Not a lot happened when I met Mother Meera," she said. "I enjoyed the stillness. It was peaceful but uneventful. It wasn't until the day after *darshan* that I had a great epiphany." Nina's friend suggested that the two of them visit the nearby town of Hadamar, the location of the Hadamar Euthanasia Center, the psychiatric hospital where the mass sterilization and murders of hundreds of thousands of people with mental and physical disabilities took place, many of them children. "We were standing in the room where the operations had been done," Nina told me, still shocked by the memory. "There was this slanted table, I'll never forget it, where vivisections were performed on the brains of psychiatric patients. On the walls were hundreds of photographs of the children who'd been killed. And near them were photos of the nurses who'd worked there. The nurses were all dressed in white peaked caps, and in one of the photos, they were standing around the führer with these beaming smiles."

She paused, then continued in disbelief. "Those nurses were so proud. They all looked so innocent. I thought to myself, 'How could these young, beautiful, robust German women be so proud of murdering children? How was that possible?' Then something clicked in my mind." Nina looked me in the eye. "This may sound strange, but as I looked at the nurses in the photograph, I started to see the absence of evil. I actually saw in that moment that everyone who commits an evil act believes they're doing the right thing. We can all be deluded in this way, under the right circumstances," she added. "It's easy to point a finger at someone who is more deluded than we are and think, 'How can that possibly be?' But the truth is that delusion exists on a spectrum."

"That doesn't excuse evil."

"No. But it helps to understand it. I went into the chapel at Hadamar and sat down. It was as if the nurses were talking to me. They said, 'We thought we were doing the right thing. Everybody believed it.' And I knew that they were telling the truth." Nina appeared to be struggling with this realization. "I was raised to believe that you don't forget and you don't forgive. Because if you forgive, you betray your ancestors. I felt like a traitor. Eighty-nine members of my family were killed in the war, that we know of. I had an intergenerational obligation to hate. But something shifted for me in that chapel."

Back at the bed-and-breakfast where she was staying, Nina listened to "Laudate Dominum" on her Walkman, an aria from Mozart's transcendent opera of praise and mercy, and began to weep. "It was as if they weren't only my tears. They were my father's unfinished tears and all the tears that were repressed in my family. Not speaking out, because if you started to grieve it would be too much. I felt these intergenerational tears moving through me and taking the hatred with them. Just letting it go. On the one hand, it felt painful, as if I were betraying my family. But on the other hand, it felt like a necessary untying of karmic knots," said Nina, who is a practicing Buddhist. "I wept for hours. It was a huge, huge release."

After Nina returned to the United States, another miracle occurred, when she created a theater piece about her experience in Germany. "My father was often not fond of my work, but to my utter surprise, he seemed to enjoy this performance," she told me. To Nina's amazement, a few months later, he booked a flight to Danzig, where he'd grown up, and which was now part of Poland. "My father swore that he would never go back. I couldn't believe it. He walked the streets of his hometown and went to visit his old high school. A woman stopped him in the hallway and asked who he was. He told her, 'I've come back.' She told him she was the principal and offered to show him around the school, and when they visited the chemistry lab, my father noticed that their copy of the periodic table was outdated and didn't include newly discovered elements. He realized how poverty-stricken the school was, and that he himself had not only survived but succeeded in a way that these Poles hadn't." Nina paused before continuing. "My father worked for the Stanford Research Institute. The first thing he did when he got back to California was to send an updated periodic table to his alma mater in Danzig. The principal wrote back to him, saying, 'I hope you know that your visit was as important to me as I imagine it was to you.' My father asked me what she could have meant by this—but he knew perfectly well. Something changed in my father after his visit. What happened to me in *darshan* had affected him as well."

●

I told Klaus, an old-timer in Mother Meera's inner circle, a little of Nina's story. "Mother shines a light," he agreed. "That is what she is doing in *darshan*, and if she sees a way that she can do more, she does." Serious and unprepossessing, Klaus may be the least starry-eyed of the close devotees, a plainspoken man temperamentally averse to spiritual ego or exaggeration. "I didn't have the Big Bang when I met Mother," he said, looking like a midlevel bureaucrat in his button-down shirt with a pen clipped into the breast pocket. "I just look at myself and ask, 'Is there a change?' And the answer is yes."

"How would you describe that change?"

"I've become more alive," Klaus said simply. "I'm more happy, more loving, and more sensitive. I feel more in harmony, too. Also stronger and more present. Connected to my inner divine, to the God inside me. That is my experience." He waited for me to draw him out further. I asked Klaus why he'd been attracted to Mother Meera in the first place. An Indian mystic who hardly speaks and offers no step-by-step formula for spiritual growth seemed an unlikely choice for a no-nonsense man like himself. Yet it was this very absence of cheesy marketing that drew him to Mother Meera, Klaus admitted. "There are gurus who tell you, 'Pay me eight hundred and fifty dollars a day and you're enlightened.' It's ridiculous. Mother has the cleanest teaching I've come across, and also the clearest, biggest connection to the Divine that I have seen. But she is never putting herself on a pedestal. She is empowering us and showing herself as a loving human being. Yet she's different."

"How so?"

He pondered this for a moment. "There is always a very strong silence around her," Klaus explained. "Some people can't handle it and they need to talk. If you are with Mother for a while, in a working situation or whatever, there is no need to speak. If one drives in a car with her, there might be silence for an hour. But it's beautiful. It's a different way of being. We are not used to it.

"Mother is not answering questions in the conceptual mind," he went on. "She's not interested in our questions about enlightenment or 'How many lives do I have left?' Her answer is always 'Why not just be happy here?' Mother is interested in this moment. If I ask her about herself or her experiences, she doesn't answer. It used to make me angry. But after a while, I realized it was a good thing that she is not answering. What can she answer?" Klaus shrugged and almost managed a smile. "Mother can put some concepts in my head. And then I will run with the concept for I don't know how long. But this is not helpful. It is more helpful what she is not saying. Instead, Mother *points*. Just look, 'she tells us.' Look who I am.' She gives the power back. She is much bigger than what is on this plane. And many people are not realizing that."

•

Sarah, an Englishwoman in her sixties, agreed that "such opportunities don't come along every day"— the chance to meet someone of Mother's ilk—though it took her "a while to catch on." A Cambridge-educated psychologist, Sarah met with me on Skype from London. She's a solid, auntlike personage, with silver hair cupping her ears in a pageboy. "I wasn't prepared for the impact she had on me when I met her in 1991," Sarah told me. "Every time I saw Mother, it was so overwhelming. It was difficult to speak, if you know what I mean."

"Trust me, I do," I assured her.

"It takes courage to overcome the fear of the divine seeing you in your entirety," Sarah said. "I have found Mother's presence sometimes so powerful that you can't think straight. Rational thought leaves you. Or you simply burst into tears. That has been one of my main problems in dealing with Mother. You burst into tears, and she just laughs at you!" Sarah looked at me through the computer screen. "Divinity has a different wavelength, doesn't it?"

"How would you describe it?"

"When I first went to see Mother, I was quite dense," Sarah replied. "I don't mean intellectually dim or slow on the uptake. I mean physically dense." Sarah slumped her shoulders like a sack of potatoes. "Through patient contact with me, on Mother's part, I have become less dense over the years. Vibrationally less slow, let's put it that way. But not constantly."

"The change has been physiological?"

"Yes," she agreed. "Most human beings are familiar with the enormous energy that comes with powerful feelings of affection or sexual entrancement. Or the mood-altering qualities of a landscape, or the thrill of a roller coaster, or the extraordinary tenderness you see when you encounter some small, endearing creature. The sight of a baby rabbit produces a different chemical reaction, doesn't it? And that chemical reaction gives rise to a physical change, an altering of the physiological makeup."

"It does."

"I'm of the opinion that if we have such a thing as a soul, it is refinable and we are here to learn that." Sarah met my eyes to make sure I was following. "This energy helps to refine us."

"And what about divine incarnation?"

"For me, a powerful indicator of Mother's true divinity is that she makes no demands of us, she makes no rules," Sarah told me. "But what she does do is sensitize us, energetically, so that we get a better understanding of our behavior and how it affects others. It could be described as an awakening of consciousness. I don't know how else to put it."

I asked Sarah if she had seen the Paramatman Light.

"No, nothing like that! I once had the experience of sitting behind the waiting chair during *darshan* and being able to feel what everybody who sat in the chair was feeling," she remembered. "It aroused such a feeling of loving compassion in me, I was astounded. I saw this lovely gold light spring between them and Mother, like an arc of a rainbow." These fleeting visions are of little importance, however. For Sarah, it is the ongoing, ordinary lessons of the heart, the tiny awakenings, that have the most lasting and powerful impact. "When something in you has truly found Mother, your life will present to you those circumstances for your best learning," she explained, sounding like the mental health professional she is. "Then you come to see what it is in yourself that you need to pay attention to."

•

I was interested in knowing how a shared devotion to Mother Meera might affect a long-term relationship, so I tracked down Ken and Elizabeth Mellor, an Australian couple who've been together for fifty-two years. An attractive, silver-haired pair in their early seventies, the Mellors are popular authors and mindfulness meditation teachers in their native Victoria and were happy to talk to me on Skype about Mother's influence on their lives.

"I was working in Switzerland, and someone gave me a book about Mother Meera in 1996," Ken started. "I had *darshan* one night and rang up Elizabeth and said, 'You've got to come over straightaway.'"

"From Australia?"

"Yes," said Elizabeth. "So I did! I came for one *darshan*, and when I saw her, I thought, 'This is absolutely worth it.'"

As connoisseurs of consciousness studies who've met and studied with many powerful teachers and gurus, the Mellors have been around the block, spiritually speaking. They have been initiated by a number of well-known meditation masters since the 1960s, yet they insist that Mother Meera's presence is wholly unique. "They were all masters of divine energy in a variety of ways. And we were familiar with the impact that someone like this can have on us," Ken told me. "But this was different. When I was sitting there, waiting for Mother to come in, about five minutes before she arrived, the energy ramped up really strongly."

"What do you mean by 'ramped up'?"

"I started to tingle all over when she was about to arrive. It was physiological," Ken said, reminding me of Sarah's story. "I felt this buildup of *potential* on the inside of me. I don't really know how else to put it. My body reacted very strongly, and then my consciousness began to expand in her presence."

Elizabeth described a similar feeling: "I had the experience of walking into the most incredible *field* with her. Even before we were inside the house. The closer I got, first of all to the village and then to the house, there was this buildup of energy. I had an intense reaction to that. I didn't know what was coming, and when she actually walked in, I had a shaking, trembling thing going on through my whole body."

"It's true," Ken agreed, backing her up.

"It was intensifying the closer she came to entering the room. When I finally saw her, my first response was 'Goodness, she's so tiny!'" Elizabeth laughed. "But her power was huge. I felt bathed through to the whole center of my being, just by her presence. There weren't any bells or whistles, just a deep, deep sense of ease, relaxation, and feeling that I was in the right place with the right person." Elizabeth paused. "Then afterward, I had intense experiences. I felt like I'd been plugged into some supercharged battery or something. I felt like I was opening up. It was incredibly beautiful."

It would be many years before the Mellors actually spoke with Mother, however. One night in 2007, they were staying at Darshan Hall, below Schloss Schaumburg, and watched as Mother was leaving for the night after *darshan*. "We poked our heads out the window to watch her go," Ken told me. "Elizabeth said, 'Good night, Mother,' and she looked up and said, 'Goodbye.' I turned to Elizabeth and said, 'Two words after eleven years. We're really getting somewhere now!'"

Elizabeth had been glad for the lack of contact. "I was so pleased that she didn't speak for a long time. It enabled me to be alone and clear in my process with her. The other teachers we'd had were talkers. It was very important for me to have that silent connection with Mother." As a mindfulness teacher, Elizabeth distrusts spiritual hierarchy of any kind. "I'm always repelled by people who get into high positions and divorce themselves from their humanity. Who present themselves as being *not people*. Although we didn't interact personally for a long time, I always saw that she was a woman—a person—as well as being a divine being."

"Her human side isn't always easy to reach, though," I countered.

Elizabeth disagreed. "She has an extreme humanness," she insisted. "That combination is fantastic for me. She's so warm and nurturing while at the same time being in this state of the divine that is incredible. And there's no separation. All of that is present for me with her. She has likes and dislikes. All of that is part of her humanity, which is very important. If she didn't show that, it would be very hard for me to actually connect with her. And because of that profound integration of the human and her divinity, she draws the same out of us."

Still, the Mellors have very different relationships to Mother Meera. Since they came to her with different needs, they have felt quite different changes in themselves. "Mother is exactly the same all the time. But her impact is unique," said Ken. "For instance, Elizabeth was born extremely premature, and like a lot of premature children, she didn't anchor herself completely in the body or the world. She had this transcendent consciousness right from the beginning. By contrast, I was raised in a very rigid Baptist tradition and was thick as a brick."

"He was," Elizabeth agreed.

"There wasn't much fluidity."

"No," she said, looking at me through the camera. "There wasn't."

"So while Elizabeth's process has been to become more grounded and in her body," Ken told me, "mine has been to become more refined and aware of the transcendent."

"And you manage to meet in the middle?" I asked.

They smiled at each other. Then at me. "We do our best," said Elizabeth.

⬩

Finally, I spoke to Kirsty MacGregor via Skype from her home in Edinburgh. A devotee of Mother's since 1992, Kirsty is a no-nonsense Scot with a wicked laugh, a hard head, and a successful career as an international consultant and speaker.

"When I first met Mother, twenty-four years ago, she was very separate from those who went to see her," Kirsty told me. "She was extremely shy, too. The first

time she came to the U.K., Mother spoke very little.
She was very happy talking to my son, who was fourteen. They had good chats, and she made his porridge
one morning. But Mother was very, very private back
then, much more enshrined and guarded. There was
always a group of people around her. Now she is much
more embodied, if that's the right word. It's almost like
she's moved towards matter—or the physical realm
has entered in her more fully. She's much more comfortable with it."

"When did that begin to change?"

"When Mother started to travel a lot," said Kirsty.
"Since then, she's had more physical contact with people outside of *darshan*. I see her engaging in a more
personal way. That has been a really big shift."

I told Kirsty what Ulrich had said about Mother
Meera being totally untouchable. She didn't seem surprised. "We all have our own experience, don't we?
A friend of mine tells me that she hugs Mother and is
physically affectionate. I have never been able to do
that." Kirsty did have a major breakthrough recently
in her relationship with Mother Meera, when she over-
came a hurdle of pride and fear. "I do *pranam* now,"
Kirsty told me, citing the practice of kneeling in front
of one's teacher and touching their feet outside of
*darshan*. "I would never have done that in the past."
While Kirsty was working at the school in India, a volunteer suggested to her—after the two of them had had
an emotional conflict—that she try doing *pranam* to
Mother. At first, she was extremely resistant. "I told
her, 'I'm not kneeling!' I'd never knelt in front of anyone in my life! The first time I saw a friend do it, I was
horrified! I thought, 'What the hell is she doing kissing

this woman's feet? Oh my God, that's really embarrassing!' It was a million miles away from my tradition. I was brought up Protestant, puritanical. Now this volunteer was telling me how beautiful and freeing it is. So I decided to try it the next day.

"I went to find Mother. She was cleaning the girls' toilets. I asked her if I could do *pranam*. She said, 'No, I'm too busy.' Later she came out of the bathroom and said no again. Now I see that she was right, I wasn't coming from the right place. I was making myself do it because I thought it would be good for me. I wasn't sincere.

"By four o'clock that afternoon, I was ready," Kirsty continued, nodding at me on Skype. "I thought, 'I'm actually ready to surrender.' This time when I asked Mother to do *pranam*, she smiled and said yes. I knelt down in front of her, touching my forehead to the ground between her feet, and found myself filled with a deeply quiet, childlike feeling of complete trust and surrender. The lift was just extraordinary!" Since then, Kirsty has been surprised by the spontaneous impulse arising within her, whenever she has seen Mother privately, to ask if she can do *pranam*. "Mother lets me because she knows my issues," Kirsty explained. "When you do it sincerely, Mother is really pleased. It's extraordinarily pure and beautiful, and it's probably the edge where I most need to be working now in my life. I would never have believed it before I did it. You go through a profound act of surrender. An act of trust, as well, that she won't abuse my being vulnerable. It's also deeply intimate. I'm bowing down to Mother Meera but also to something *other*, not to her personality, but this energy. It's both personal and impersonal."

Earlier in life, Kirsty had worked at Brockwood Park, Jidda Krishnamurti's school in England, and received a corresponding lesson from K himself. One day during a discussion with the staff, Kirsty remembered, "Krishnaji said to me, 'You have to learn to become totally vulnerable.' That was important for me to hear. Vulnerability means surrender. It's undefended. You're surrendering the part of you that is a construct, the egoic thing that's holding on to its identity for survival. That's what Krishnaji was saying. Do you know what I mean?" she asked.

"All too well," I assured her.

"Then," Kirsty said with a knowing smile, "the whole thing begins to shift."

# LEARNING TO LISTEN

Those weeks near Schloss Schaumburg were a time out of time, blessedly peaceful, reflective, and silent. I woke every morning before dawn and shuffled down to the *darshan* room, where I'd sit for an hour, meditating in front of Mother Meera's empty chair. I'd been struggling with so many unanswered questions and still didn't know how to write about Mother. Something was eluding me. I had hoped our time together in India would reveal this missing piece, yet I'd left Madanapalle more mystified than before. Every time I thought I had it, Mother's story turned to mercury, slipped through my fingers, and disappeared. I'd written and thrown away a hundred-plus pages, talked to dozens of devotees around the world, ransacked my journals for forgotten details, pored through transcripts of interviews I'd done with her dating back to the 1980s in the hope of catching this missing thread, but the book would not materialize. I had even spoken to Andrew about Mother—a confrontation I'd avoided for fifteen years—and was reassured to hear that Andrew had long ago forgiven whatever had happened between him and Mother. "I'm sure there are people that Meera can help," Andrew admitted. Still, the book that Mother Meera encouraged me to write remained unfinished. I'd sit there every morning in the *darshan* room, meditating in front of her chair in the dark, waiting for a sign about what to do next. But nothing emerged.

Finally, left with no other choice, I decided to stop pushing so hard and to turn this conundrum over to God, so to speak. I remembered Adilakshmi's advice in India—"Find out what she is trying to teach you"— and was doing my best to follow her lead. Having come to the end of my stay at Darshan Hall, I had no idea where all this was headed. Might it be that Mother's story was too enigmatic to cohere in a conventional narrative? Was I locked in a creative conundrum to do with some shortage of writerly skill? Or was this, in fact, a problem of faith? Maybe a person with so little faith simply could not do her story justice. I'd done my best to keep an open mind, to be sensitive to views I did not share, to maintain a willing suspension of disbelief in the presence of mysteries I could not explain. As for faith, I kept a hopeful line from Tagore nearby as a model for how to think about this: "Faith is the bird that feels the light and sings while the dawn is still dark." I realized that the poet must be right, and yet I had not managed to sing. The song itself seemed beyond my reach.

The day before I was to leave—June 14, 2015— after an especially peaceful sitting, I opened my eyes and felt the urge to do *pranam* in front of Mother Meera's chair. I'd done this only once before, shortly after meeting her thirty-one years prior, and now, after hearing Kirsty's story, I decided to follow the impulse

again. Making sure that no one else was around, I
stepped up to the empty chair, knelt down, and laid my
forehead on the white cushion where Mother Meera
rests her feet. Instantly, my ears were filled with that
same buzzing I'd first heard in the foyer of Mother's
house the night I arrived there with Andrew. I stayed
where I was for several minutes, enjoying the pleasant fizzing sensation the sound elicited inside my body.
I emptied my mind as I knelt there, till eventually a
prayer appeared: I asked to be shown what I needed to
know in order to push through this present darkness. I
surrendered to the urge to kiss the cushion; then stood
up feeling light-headed and calm, and slowly made my
way back to my room.

I had no intention of writing that day and had
planned to spend the morning hiking up into the forest behind the *Schloss*. Nor had I attempted to talk to
Mother Meera; I was done with trying to force that
issue. She'd given no indication that she wanted to
cooperate and it was a relief to have dropped the struggle. From my bedroom window, I looked down at the
walled-in park on the side of Darshan Hall, brushed
now with light from the morning sun. Rather than
have breakfast and venture out for my hike, though,
I felt the urge to turn on my computer, to read back
over the stalled manuscript. I put my fingers on the
keyboard and waited. The lawn was turning emerald
green; the birds were landing to drink up the dew. Not
a sound could be heard from where I was sitting. I
stared at the blank computer screen. Then a phantom
rose up in my memory.

It was fifteen years earlier, in the dead of winter.
I'd been living in Mother Meera's house for three long,

frustrating months, wrestling with another book, the memoir about death and enlightenment. The German winter had been dreary and endless; day after day, I sat at my desk, listening to rainwater pour down the drainpipe, hardly able to write a word. As now, there was some insurmountable barrier standing between me and the story I wanted to tell. I'd been grinding my gears but getting nowhere, and ached to pack my bags and leave. Each time I planned to go, however, I would hear Mother Meera's voice in the hall or catch sight of her outside in her parka and mud boots, and think, "Where do you think you're running to?" I had no family or home to go back to; I was free to stay there as long as I liked. My anxiety was a clear indication that I was approaching something that scared me. I could choose to escape from this pressure cooker, fleeing back into the blur of life, but I'd miss the opportunity to grow through this darkness and learn what it was that I needed to know. So I stayed in Thalheim, week after week, waiting for the fog to lift and this frightening thing to revel itself.

One especially bleak afternoon, I was typing at my computer when an inexplicable thing occurred. Out of nowhere, a stream of invisible "liquid"—syrupy, gentle, and warm—began to drip onto the top of my head. The sensation was soothing and weirdly hypnotic; my eyelids felt heavy and wanted to close. I resisted the urge to sink into this stupor, as if it were a vat of honey, and forced myself to get back to work. When I began again to type, a voice whispered into my ear: "Stop." I assumed my mind was playing tricks on me and pushed myself to keep on typing as this nectar continued to fall from above. Once again, the voice told me to *stop*. I ignored it, focused on what I was writing, and it was then that the most "supernatural" thing in my life to date took place: My computer keyboard went dead. I'd been working on it for hours when it suddenly *stopped* for no apparent reason, and could not be revived. I tried to stand up, to shake off the weirdness, but found that I was stuck to my chair like an insect in a pool of amber. Golden syrup seemed to have hardened around me, yet although I could not move a muscle, my vision was perfectly lucid and clear.

In my mind's eye, I saw Mother enter the room, seemingly real and physically present. She walked toward me, lowered her head, and rested her forehead flat against mine. I could actually feel our skin touch; then she said, "Remember that I love you." Mother pulled away from me and instantly I was overwhelmed by a nightmarish film, an ugly montage of pictures from my childhood, flashing before me in 3-D—scenes of abandonment, suicide, rapes, forced isolation, and heartless betrayals; a horror show of ancient memories shot through with trauma and primitive loss. Beyond this visual onslaught, I heard myself screaming my own mother's name as if from behind a cemented door, a no-man's-land where no one could hear me. I realized that I was completely alone; my mother was long gone and would never come back. As this thought crossed my mind, I felt something crack in the back of my chest, like a bone being shifted and set back in place.

When the episode ended, I opened my eyes; I was facedown on the floor with one arm wrapped around my stomach and the other hand stuffed in a ball in my mouth. The left side of my body was completely numb. I couldn't move for several minutes. Then I heard Mother's voice again in my ear: "Remember that I love you." I knew in my gut what this vision meant, the warning she was trying to send me. *As long as you believe that this is what being a child means, you will never surrender to life. You will never feel at home in the world or open your heart without fear to another. You will never feel comfortable in your own skin, recognize your essential goodness, or experience your connection to God. You will never love completely.*

That was my secret truth, after all, the terror that had blocked me ever since I could remember—emotionally, creatively, and spiritually. Long before I could give voice to these things, the prospect of being a helpless child had fused with terror and loss in my psyche. Before I knew what was happening, I'd vowed not to be like a child again *ever*—unguarded, dependent, trusting, naive—thinking that this would destroy me. Yet as long as I feared this humble perspective, the orphan inside me would never be free. I could never fully embrace the unknown or remain open to the divine. Instead, I would remain an impostor—defensive, paranoid, sometimes hard-hearted—fearing that if I dropped the mask, or allowed myself to care too much, a malicious shadow would swallow me up.

Now, looking out from my room at Schloss Schaumburg, I grasped what had happened in India. After years of hiding from Mother Meera, I'd finally allowed myself to trust her and come to Madanapalle in need of her help. In return, she'd rejected me—brutally, it seemed to me—and left me feeling like an orphan again, exiled from the circle of love (as when I'd seen her playing with the ashram kids). I'd convinced myself that this orphan was gone, only to realize how fraught he still was, trapped inside my emotional body. This was the lesson that Mother had taught me. The upshot of her message was clear: *If you want to write a book about me, you will need to learn about trust. You will need to begin to surrender. You'll need to be like a child again if you hope to approach the question of God. And if you want to tell my story.*

A wave of lightness swept over me; the truth transported my mind and spirit. There would be no final closure to healing, I realized, and that was exactly as it should be. Unless our wounds remain slightly open, we begin to forget how tender we are. We can't possibly understand holiness without remembering the depth of our own pain, the separation we feel from God. How else can one hope to write about someone whose life is devoted to suffering's end? Without dropping the remnants of my own armor, how could I begin to understand her? I realized that this was the missing piece—the step I wanted so badly to skip—the block that kept me from proceeding. For the first time in many months, I suddenly felt the urge to write. I turned on my computer, sketched out these thoughts, and didn't stop working for two hours straight. I finally knew, without any doubt, that this mysterious book could be written.

•

At *darshan* that evening, I sat in the back row next to Herbert. I felt no need to rush up and see Mother or let her know that I was leaving the next day. I was perfectly content to watch from afar; there was nothing grabbing or pushing inside me. I felt no craving for something more; nor did there seem to be anything missing. Nothing to seek and nowhere to get to. When my turn came, I crawled toward Mother Meera and put my head between her hands. I felt nothing, as usual, when she touched my temples and examined me with her dark eyes. Afterward, I sat in my seat, knowing that there'd been a seminal shift. I passed Daniel in the lobby on the way out; he winked and nodded his head, as if to tell me he could see it.

●

The following morning, I wrote a goodbye note to Mother Meera. I wanted to let her know that I'd finally figured out what was blocking me and now understood how to tell her story. I included a favorite quotation that described how this breakthrough felt to me. It was from *The Sparkling Stone*, a collection of meditations by John van Ruysbroeck, a Flemish mystic, published around the year 1340:

> When love has carried us above all things...
> we receive in peace the Incomprehensible
> Light, enfolding and penetrating us. What
> is this Light, if it be not a contemplation
> of the Infinite, and an intuition of eternity?

I folded the note into a parchment envelope and planned to hand it off to Herbert or Daniel before I left, in the hope that it would find its way to Mother. Not two minutes later, there was a knock at the door, so faint I almost didn't hear it. It was Bettina, one of Mother's helpers, asking if I could come for a visit.

Mother wanted to see me, she said. Could I meet her downstairs at eleven o'clock? Absolutely, I assured her. I couldn't believe this was happening *now*. Bettina bowed at the waist, turned on her heel, and disappeared down the long blue hallway.

Was this some kind of cosmic joke? I ironed a shirt and found my notes. At the stroke of eleven, I met Bettina in the parking lot and followed her down the mountain in my rental car, past the town of Diez, over the Lahn River, and along a series of country roads till the Thalheim church spire came into view. I tailed her through the familiar streets till we came to Mother's driveway. Bettina opened the door and we climbed the stairs to Mother's apartment. There were three tiny pairs of shoes on the doormat. "We're here, Ma!" Bettina called out. Mother opened the door, looked me straight in the eye, and told Bettina she could go.

She was unusually dressed-up that day, in a rose-colored sari, carefully pressed, with her hair cascading over one shoulder, more salt and pepper than I had realized. Mother offered me a seat on the sofa and took a straight-backed chair for herself.

She surprised me by inquiring about my work. "How is the book going?" Mother asked.

I told her that the last two days had been my most productive in months. She smiled and said, "This is good." I reached into my pocket for a tape recorder, but Mother requested that I not use it. Instead, I pulled out a notebook and a list of questions, half of which I'd already crossed out. Mother seemed to be watching me with a look of amusement. Or was it affection? The light was hitting her feline eyes, turning them a bright hazel. The frightening Mother from India was gone for the moment. Now there was simply this gracious woman, smiling, relaxed, and strangely familiar. For the first time in all the years I'd known her, I felt perfectly at ease with Mother Meera. We chatted together about this and that, my health, the global water shortage, the school in Madanapalle. Then Mother said, "You may ask your questions."

I picked up my notebook and pen. "Thank you, Mother. First, let me say that I know you're a very private person."

"No, I am *public*," she corrected me. Mother seemed to be teasing.

"Okay, then," I replied. "Can you tell me what it was like for you, being a little girl? Is Kamala Reddy still inside you?"

"I never think about it," Mother replied.

"Was it strange for you to know who you were, and where you came from? When you were still a child?"

She looked quizzical.

"Do you understand what I'm asking?"

"People could see I was different," she said. "Even when I was young."

"Do you mean your parents?"

"Everybody."

"What did your parents think about you?"

"We were never close," Mother said. There was no sign of regret in her voice.

I told her that I'd seen her mother, Antamma, at the school in India. She was a stick-thin, kind-faced woman who'd done *pranam* in front of Mother like everyone else at *darshan*. "I wonder what she thought about her daughter," I asked. "Knowing what she had brought into the world. Was she surprised?"

Mother Meera said, "She treats me with respect." Clearly, this subject didn't interest her.

"What about Mr. Reddy?" I said. "What would your life have been like without him? If the two of you had never met?"

Mother considered this. "It was fate," she said.

"Do you mean you couldn't *not* have met him?"

"I recognized him and he recognized me."

There was nothing more to be said about it. I related to Mother my understanding that Mr. Reddy's death had caused her great pain. "Is it hard not having him around to talk to?" I asked.

"Just because he is not in a body doesn't mean I cannot talk to him." She sounded completely serious.

"And do you still have the kinds of experiences you used to share only with Mr. Reddy?"

"Yes," she replied.

"It must have been a great help having him around when you were young. Knowing that he believed you."

"If God's grace is there, all is well. If it is not there, what good is it to ask anyone for help?" Mother said, as if this were an answer to my question.

"You make that sound so simple," I told her.

"God is simple. It is humans who complicate things."

The ways she said "humans" was odd to the ear. "And the paintings you did of Mr. Reddy's soul after he died. Is that what you actually saw?" I asked, thinking of those visionary pictures, figures flowing together through the prismlike air. This series of spontaneous canvases is the only glimpse we have into what Mother sees—and how she sees it.

She nodded.

"That's amazing, Mother."

"No. It is normal."

I took a chance. "Can you tell me what you see when you look at me now?"

Mother glanced at the space above my head. "I see your struggles. And also your challenges."

"Do these correspond to the knots you untie during *darshan*?"

She looked at me without speaking. I longed to ask her more about this but continued with the questions I'd prepared. "Would you say that you have good days and bad days? On a personal level?"

"Only in India." Mother grinned.

"I'd never seen you get angry before."

"In work situations only. I must shout sometimes. It must be done. But it is not my character."

"It's in your character to feel emotions, though?"

"Yes," Mother said. "For an avatar, also, there is pain. I must bear it."

"Do you ever feel fear?" I asked.

"I am never afraid," she told me. "I used to love going out alone in the dark. When I was a child. People said it was dangerous because there were scorpions everywhere. But it never frightened me."

"Are you afraid of dying, Mother?"

"No," she said lightly.

We talked about the state of the world and the challenges facing human beings. "There's so much danger and fear," I said. "When it comes to injustice, when is it right to fight back? To use anger? To take action in the service of the good?"

"When your heart is clear, you may act," Mother said. "Otherwise, you only make things worse."

"Isn't it better to do something than nothing at all?" I wondered. "Even if your heart's not completely clear?"

"The destruction of the world is a human idea. Not a divine one," she replied.

"Many people are terrified. They think the world is about to end."

Mother Meera corrected this: "Humanity will not be destroyed. There is nothing to fear."

*I hope you're right*, I thought to myself. There were a hundred more questions I wanted to ask but our conversation had come to a stop. We sat quietly for a couple of minutes. For once, I was not overwhelmed by her silence; my brain hadn't melted or turned to mush. I could have sat there with her for the rest of the day, in fact, and never said another word. What more was there to ask her, really? Except, perhaps, one more thing.

"I have one last question, Mother."

She looked at me.

"Will you ever come again?" The words sounded strange coming out of my mouth. "Will you have another... incarnation?"

"I do not know," Mother Meera answered. "It depends on Paramatman. And also on the wishes and prayers of devotees. For me to be born again."

I had the sudden urge in that moment to do *pranam* in front of her. I remembered Kirsty's story about the importance of being ready, though, and held back from asking Mother's permission. "Maybe next time," I thought to myself. I thanked Mother Meera for asking to see me, told her it meant the world to me. She seemed to know this already.

"Call if you need me," Mother said. I promised her that I'd stay in touch, waited for her to stand up first, then followed her back out to the hallway. Resisting the urge to touch her shoulder, I put my hand on my heart instead. Mother looked at me with great love in her eyes. "Will I ever know who you are?" I thought when she turned and went back into her kitchen, leaving the door ajar behind her. I walked carefully down the white marble stairs and glanced back over my shoulder, once, to see that the door was still open. Then I stepped out into the glorious morning.

# AFTERWORD

Late one August afternoon in 1991, Andrew Harvey and I were invited to hear a talk at the New Camaldoli monastery in Big Sur, California. The speaker was Father Bede Griffiths, a Benedictine monk and author who'd devoted his life to founding a Christian-Hindu ashram in South India, and to a rapprochement among the world's mystic traditions. Knowing Father Bede from his writings, I was taken aback upon entering the small chapel by his otherworldly beauty, gaunt as an El Greco saint, snowy-haired in a saffron robe. In flawless Oxbridge tones,. Father Bede proceeded to speak for an hour on a topic that didn't interest me much—prayer in daily life, I think—then he turned, unexpectedly, to a recent experience that had shattered his own spiritual life.

Seated outside his ashram hut one morning, Father Bede told us, he had suddenly been knocked to the ground by an unseen force while he was praying. Frightened, the eighty-four-year-old monk managed to crawl to his bed, where he remained for a week in a semiconscious state, attended to by a team of doctors unable to diagnose his condition. Finally, after ten days, the doctors gave up hope and Father Bede was given his last rites. A short time later, as he lay there dying, a voice came to him with a message. "Remember the Mother," the voice said. Father Bede recovered shortly thereafter.

I found this confession extraordinary. Here was one of the great mystic pioneers of our time, a devout Christian who'd spent the past fifty years working toward spiritual reform, admitting a major oversight in his faith. "It is the Mother," Father Bede went on to say, who animates the whole of creation. It is the Mother whose grace is so sorely needed by the church, to help it enfold a suffering world, to quiet its fundamentalism, to dissolve its bureaucracies, and to heal our ailing planet.

After the talk was finished, Andrew and I sat on a cliff overlooking the Pacific. The sun had nearly set behind a bank of golden clouds. We watched as the light played on the dark water, but felt no need to speak. "All of this is the Mother," I thought, remembering what Father Bede had said. I imagined us floating in her glass belly, gazing out onto a magical world of fantastic colors, shapes, and adornments, being given an experience of what a moment in her body might feel like, the rapture of it. The boulders jutting up from the black water, the eucalyptus trees, the gulls and pelicans and seals squalling in the increasing dark: all these things revealed themselves to me as part of her in that moment. This wasn't metaphorical thinking but a tangible presence, a sensory suffusion. I was breathing her—being carried inside her breath; the world appeared to expand and contract with the movement of my own lungs. When Andrew left, I stayed there for a long time, staring out into this natural heaven.

I started this book with a simple question: How does a person choose to respond when confronted with incomprehensible things, aspects of reality we can't fathom—the transcendental, the unearthly, the ineffable? Do we withdraw to our familiar corners, closing our eyes to evidence of the unseen world, or open ourselves to mystery and the overwhelming evidence of how little we actually know? This is, indeed, the most important choice any of us will make in a lifetime: question or withdraw, reveal or conceal, venture out or stay fixed in our views, denying what we are afraid to explore. "The saint is one who knows that every moment of our human life is a moment of crisis," Aldous Huxley wrote. "For at every moment we are called upon to make an all-important decision—to choose between the way that leads to death and spiritual darkness and the way that leads towards light and life." Stepping through the door that Mother had opened, moving toward this invisible realm, I had chosen life and light. When I made that choice, my worldview was transformed. Today, I'm no longer as cynical about using the word "God," either, since it doesn't matter what we call it. As long as we admit that this power is there or, if we haven't glimpsed it ourselves, are willing to be shown.

"The greatest scientists are humble because they are used to what they cannot see," Mother Meera tells us. "And because what they are discovering is revealing mystery after mystery to them." Humility and wonder go hand in hand. Without humility, the

willingness to be shown, the world goes flat, predict-
able, wrong. The mind holds sway, the spirit sags, and
the mystical passes us by without notice. We shrink to
fit into what we're not afraid of; life comes to seem far
smaller than it is. We forget that we're children of this
great Mother, floating inside her miraculous belly. Far
from being unscientific, this awareness is "the sower
of all true science," as Albert Einstein affirmed. "The
most beautiful and most profound emotion we can
experience is the sensation of the mystical," the father
of relativity believed. "He to whom this emotion is a
stranger, who can no longer wonder and stand rapt in
awe, is as good as dead."

There are signs and wonders, if we keep our eyes
open. Creation is a field of light.

# ACKNOWLEDGMENTS

My deepest gratitude to Mother Meera and those close to her for their help with this book: Adilakshmi Olati, Kirsty MacGregor, Herbert Bednarz, Daniel Toplak, Michael Zarthe, and Tony Akkanen. Thank you, too, to the many devotees who shared their stories with me in India, Germany, and the United States.

To my extraordinary editor, Cindy Spiegel, whose faith and support have been such a gift; to Joy Harris, my beloved agent, thank you for twenty-five years of friendship; and to my friend Sharyl Volpe, whose help in preparing this manuscript has been indispensable.

Finally, to the family and friends who've kept me afloat along the way: Barbara Graham, Florence Falk, Robert Levithan, Eve Ensler, Gwenyth Jackaway, Martha Cooley, Catherine Ingram, Karen Fuchs, Gary Lennon, James Lecesne, Michael Klein, Joe Dolce, Jill Angelo, Belle Heil, Martin Shanker, Jeanne Demers, Nina Wise, Naomi Shragai, Trisha Coburn, and Andrew Harvey. Deep bows.

And most of all to David Moore, my partner in all things. *Amor est spiritus qui nos alet.*

# SELECTED BIBLIOGRAPHY

Anandamayi Ma. *Matri Darshana*, Mangalam Verlag and Schang. Germany, 1983.

Buechner, Frederick. *Listening to Your Life: Daily Meditations with Frederic Buechner*, HarperCollins, New York, 1992.

Einstein, Albert. *Autobiographical Notes*, Open Court, Chicago, IL, 1979.

Eucken, Rudolf. *The Life of the Spirit*, G. P. Putnam's Sons, New York, 1909.

Ghose, Aurobindo. *Essays on the Gita*, Sri Aurobindo Ashram Trust, Pondicherry, 1995.

———. *The Life Divine*, Sri Aurobindo Ashram Trust, Pondicherry, 1951.

Goodman, Martin. *In Search of the Divine Mother*, Thorson's, London, 1998.

Hallstrom, Lisa. *Mother of Bliss: Anandamayi Ma*, Oxford University Press, New York, 1999.

Howard, Alice and Walden. *Exploring the Road Less Traveled*, Simon & Schuster, New York, 1985.

Harvey, Andrew. *Hidden Journey: A Spiritual Awakening*, Henry Holt, New York, 1991.

Harvey, Andrew, and Anne Baring. *The Divine*

*Feminine: Exploring the Feminine Face of God Throughout the World*, Conari Press, Newburyport, MA, 1996.

Harvey, Andrew, and Mark Matousek. *Dialogues with a Modern Mystic*, Quest Publishers, Wheaton, IL, 1994.

Huxley, Aldous. *The Perennial Philosophy*, Harper & Brothers, New York, 1945.

Isherwood, Christopher. *Ramakrishna and His Disciples*, Vedanta Press, Los Angeles, 1965.

Lutyens, Mary. *The Life and Death of Krishnamurti*, Krishnamurti Foundation Trust, Brockwood, U.K., 2003.

Meera, Mother. *Answers: Part I*, Mother Meera Foundation, Dornburg-Thalheim, Germany, 1991.

———. *Answers: Part II*, Mother Meera Foundation, Dornburg-Thalheim, Germany, 1991.

———. *Bringing Down the Light: Journey of a Soul After Death*, Meeramma Publications, Ithaca, NY, 1990.

Meher Baba. *The Discourses*, Sheriar Press, Myrtle Beach, SC, 1987.

Olati, Adilakshmi. *The Mother*, Mother Meera Foundation, Dornburg-Thalheim, Germany, 1987.

Rilke, Rainer Maria. *Letters to a Young Poet*, W.W. Norton, New York, 1934.

Ruusbroec, John. *The Spiritual Espousals, The Sparkling Stone, and Other Works*, The Paulist Press, New York, 1986.

Satprem. *Sri Aurobindo, or The Adventure of Consciousness*, CreateSpace Independent Publisher Platform, New York, 2015.

Shearer, Alistair, and Peter Russell, trans. *The Upanishads*, Bell Tower Books, New York, 1978.

Tolle, Eckhart. *The Power of Now: A Guide to Spiritual Enlightenment*, New World Library, Novato, CA, 1999.

Underhill, Evelyn. *Mysticism*, E. P. Dutton, New York, 1990.

# ABOUT THE AUTHOR

MARK MATOUSEK is the author of two acclaimed memoirs, *Sex Death Enlightenment: A True Story* (an international bestseller) and *The Boy He Left Behind: A Man's Search for His Lost Father*, as well as *Lessons From an American Stoic: How Emerson Can Change Your Life*, *When You're Falling, Dive: Lessons in the Art of Living*, and *Ethical Wisdom: The Search for a Moral Life*. A former editor at *Interview* magazine, he is a featured blogger for Psychology Today.com and the Huffington Post, and has contributed to numerous anthologies and publications, including *The New Yorker, O: The Oprah Magazine* (contributing editor), *Harper's Bazaar, Yoga Journal, Tricycle: The Buddhist Review*, and *The Saturday Evening Post*. A popular speaker and teacher, he offers courses in creativity and spiritual growth in the United States, Canada, Australia, and Europe, based on his book, *Writing to Awaken: A Journey of Truth, Transformation, and Self-Discovery*. A founding member of V-Men (with Eve Ensler), a movement devoted to ending violence against women and girls, he lives and works in East Hampton, New York.

9 781958 972236